Fred DeRuvo

Copyright © 2009 by Adroit Publications

All rights reserved. Written permission must be secured from the author to use or reproduce any part of this book, except brief quotations in critical reviews or articles.

Published in Scotts Valley, California, by Adroit Ventures, Inc.
www.adroitpublications.com • www.rightly-dividing.com

Scripture quotations (unless otherwise noted) are from The Holy Bible, English Standard Version®, copyright © 2001 by Crossway Bibles, a publishing ministry of Good News Publishers. Used by permission. All rights reserved.

Images used in this publication (unless otherwise noted) are from clipartconnection.com and used with permission, ©2007 JUPITERIMAGES, and its licensors. All rights reserved.

All Woodcuts used herein are in the Public Domain and free of copyright.

Library of Congress Cataloging-in-Publication Data

DeRuvo, Fred, 1957 –

ISBN 1442100818
EAN-13 9781442100817

1. Religion – Biblical Studies – General

Foreword

This book was difficult to write for a number of reasons. It was difficult because there was so much research that needed to be done in the area of the "ex-Christian" and atheist. These folks, by and large, are not sympathetic to Christianity or religion in general. In fact, many of them are simply mean-spirited, making inflammatory remarks for no other reason than they can.

For these people, not only are Christians wrong, but irrational, deluded and worse. While I have developed a thick skin for myself, I have not, nor ever will have the same thickness of skin where my Lord and Savior is concerned. What fools speak about Him under the guise of "knowledge" is nothing more than thinly disguised contempt for the One who died in order that they might have eternal life.

I do not care what I am called, or how I am viewed by the world. What I care about (and will rise to defend) is how Jesus is seen and what He is called. One type of defense comes in the form of this book.

Years ago, I saw a bumper sticker that read "Sarcasm: Just Another Service I Offer." It has become one of my favorite sayings outside of Scripture because at my core, sarcasm is my second language. In fact, if not kept in check, it could easily become my first language. I do my best to keep it in check, but there are times, as the reader will note, that I simply choose to let it out. I hope that the reader will forgive those occurrences, but sarcasm can often make the truth plainer than anything else.

I hope you will gain something from this book. I hope that you will be encouraged to do your own research. I hope ultimately though, that you will realize the futility and foolishness of those who say that God does not exist, and that you will come to see the truth. May the Lord be gracious to you and may He open your eyes to the truth that only exists in Him.

Before I forget, many thanks to Bob and Kristin Thompson; Kristin for all her editing efforts and Bob for his encouraging demeanor! You both are a blessing!

- Fred DeRuvo
April, 2009

Contents

Chapter 1: An Ex-Christian 6

Chapter 2: The Spiritual Transaction 34

Chapter 3: Richness of the Soil 43

Chapter 4: Look Alikes and Copy Cats 49

Chapter 5: Freedom to Be 59

Chapter 6: A Bite in Malta 126

Chapter 7: Missed It By That Much! 140

Chapter 8: Prove It! 170

Chapter 9: The Only Path of Truth 177

Chapter 10: Society for the Abuse of Moral Freedom 187

Chapter 11: Walking Through the Old Testament 199

Chapter 12: Hello, I'm Margaret MacDonald 209

Chapter 13: Will All Christians Fly Away En Masse? 216

Chapter 14: Slaves in Egypt 230

Notes and Listing of Resources 238

To Jesus Christ: Savior, Lord, God and King:

God is either fully sovereign or He is not. Based on the biblical as well as extra-biblical evidence, it can only be rationally concluded that He is fully sovereign.

God is <u>not</u> dependent upon, nor hindered by anything outside of Himself in order to, by any means He sees fit, bring glory to Himself.

God is holy, all powerful, all knowing and perfect. There is no one beside Him, and there is no one who can voluntarily stand in His presence. Certainly, there is no other God but Him; one God in three distinct Personalities.

I am thankful for salvation. I am grateful that He chose me for His salvation, before the foundations of the world, in the determinate council of the Godhead, from eternity past.

It is my prayer that the remainder of my life on earth would bring nothing but praise, glory and honor to God, my heavenly Father.

Chapter 1

There is something extremely interesting occurring and it appears to be occurring in large numbers. There is a growing number of people who classify themselves as "ex-Christians." They say they no longer believe in Jesus Christ as any type of mediator or God for humanity. Many of them now believe that absolutely no God exists at all, having become atheists.

Just exactly what is going on in the world today that is creating this phenomenon? Should we be surprised? Should we wonder if there is something wrong with Christianity? Is there a correlation between what these folks now think and believe and possibly what they may have gone through while involved in church?

It seems reasonable and necessary to address this situation, if for no other reason than to find out what these folks are thinking; to determine what is going on in their heads.

In response to an email in which I indicated my confusion regarding the situation he now found himself in, one individual put it like this:

"I'll make it real simple for you...

"I'm not only now an atheist, having once been a deep believer, but I once believed in Santa Claus and then later came to see that my belief in Ole' St. Nick was unfounded. The same is true of my belief in Jesus. Being a Christian means BELIEVING the Christian story. But as with all stories, it is possible to come to believe in something else. I no longer believe those old stories. Instead, I believe in reason.

"Exactly what about this is the slightest bit confusing?"

The above paragraph brings an interesting definition of Christianity to the fore. Please note that this individual states he was a "deep believer" and uses the phrase "Being a Christian means BELIEVING the Christian story" to define Christianity. Really? This is the definition of being a Christian: believing the Christian story? What exactly does that entail? Most importantly, if we relegate our research to the Bible only, are we safe?

You would think we would be, but even there we can come across a number of what we might consider to be "irregularities" unless we take the time to purposefully search the entire Bible throughout in order to make absolute sense of what W. Graham Scroggie and others have called the "Unfolding Drama of Redemption."

Works-Based

Most of us are well aware that two people can read the same part of the Bible and come away with two completely different understandings. They can also come away with a completely different meaning than the one God intended it to relay.

For instance, someone reading the Beatitudes might come to believe that Christ is teaching a works-based salvation. Just do this or that, do them well, and salvation is yours. Another person reading the same text understands it to say something else not related to salvation. Another individual might read another part of the New Testament and determine that in order to be absolutely sure of having received salvation, one must believe *and* be baptized. This again is works-based, but it is narrower in focus. Nonetheless, it is still works-based and just as wrong as the individual's conclusions after reading the Beatitudes.

Another might read yet a different part of the New Testament and determine that salvation comes by faith in Jesus as Savior. It is obvious that for our friend just quoted, being a Christian meant believing a story.

So then, by that rationale, if I believe in Batman® with all my heart; I begin to pray to Batman, imitate him and do all the things that Batman does and has done in the comic books, does that make Batman a real person?

By the same token, if I choose to believe that God does *not* exist and beyond this life there is absolutely nothing, does that make it so? God's existence (or not) does not in any way, shape or form depend upon an individual's ability to believe strongly one way or another. Either God exists or He does not exist. It cannot be both ways.

But what about the ex-Christian? Is there something that Christians are missing that has beguiled and confused them so that their spiritual eyesight is covered, keeping them deluded in the dark? Is Christianity something that is merely *thought* and *believed* to be true, but in reality, is not only *not* true, but more to the point, is a complete waste of time?

Does being a Christian mean that one simply *does* certain things, or *acts* in a certain way which causes others (and even that person himself) to believe his salvation to be true? Or, is this all there is to being a Christian; *merely believing in the story about Jesus?* It is of absolute importance to come to terms with these questions and others like them, in order to fully comprehend what is at stake here.

Either the ex-Christian has it correct (or maybe more accurately, the atheist), or the actual Christian does. It obviously cannot be both, any more than Christianity and all other religions represent many paths to the same God.

Christianity stands in diametric opposition to every other religious system, allowing no room for common ground, which is also a factor in seeing a supposed moral arrogance on the part of the Christian. Christianity stands alone, offering what no other religious system offers: a guarantee of eternal life, obtained through God's grace, by faith in the redemptive work of Jesus Christ *alone*. There is NO other religious system which claims what Christianity claims and certainly no other religious system in which the founder claimed to die so that others might live, and by His death, offers salvation to those who will be saved.

But What IS an Ex-Christian?
Before getting too deeply into the differences between Christians and non (or ex) Christians, it will helpful to define the term "ex-Christian" so that we are all on the same page. It will also be useful to provide reasons *why* ex-Christians consider themselves to have been Christians at all.

It seems that an "ex-Christian" by their own definition is a person who *used to be* a Christian, but is no longer. You would think that would be self-explanatory and obvious, however it gives rise to other questions. Simply put, it fails to address the question of any *spiritual transaction* that the Bible says takes place for that individual who claims to no longer be a Christian, but once was. The emphasis given as part of the definition is what is *done (or thought) by the person claiming to be a Christian* which initially caused them believe themselves to be a Christian.

Another individual elaborated a bit more by stating *"...Used to believe the Bible was the word of God. That Jesus died for my sins. Baptized, sanctified, purified, washed in the blood of the Lamb. One of the chosen. Friend of Jesus. Approved by GOD."* This is certainly more in depth and specific, yet it only again highlights what the person did or believed which could have been nothing more than head knowledge.

Is there anything else that can be applied to this definition, which will shed more light on the scope of meaning as applied to the ex-Christian?

Interestingly enough, this same person went a bit further by declaring: *"Now, I **know** it was all a big mind game and that none of it is real."* (emphasis mine)

So, having once *believed* that the Bible was God's Word, and that Jesus died for his sins, etc., he now *knew* that it had absolutely no basis in truth of any kind. How was this person only able to *believe* something, yet was able to finally come to a supposed *actual knowledge* of its falsehood later? The answer is very simple, but it is something that every ex-Christian will bristle at hearing. They will state without equivocation (and usually with some amount of volume) their abject disagreement when told they never were in fact Christians at all.

Of course it will be beneficial to remember that we are not truly capable of knowing what is actually going on in our hearts. The Bible states *"The heart is deceitful above all things, and it is desperately sick: who can know it?"* (Jeremiah 17:9)

No one likes to be told anything contrary to what they believe about their own life. After all, how could anyone *outside* that person truly know their inner workings? Certainly this argument has merit and it is something that the Bible intimates as well in various places. No one can ultimately know what goes on in the heart or mind of another individual. Even people who have been married for decades still find something new about their mate, which often tends to surprise them.

But it is interesting that this particular author was told in no uncertain terms by a current ex-Christian that *all Christians are merely professing Christians* because it is impossible to know otherwise. So, it is actually impossible for a Christian to know whether or not he is a Christian, according to this individual. Yet, this same person has no qualms about stating unequivocally that he <u>knows</u> "it was all a big mind game..." That is interesting. On one hand, the Christian is expected to yield to his 'unerring' rationale which states that it is impossible to know whether one is or is not truly a Christian, yet this same rationale is not applied to him when it comes to whether or not he can *know* that Christianity is true or not. That certainly seems like a double standard if ever there was one.

The Wonder of the World

From the world's point of view, statements like the ones quoted above are easily understood. After all, the world sees *no reality* in Christianity over other religions and often sees no religion as being viable. The world sees nothing inherently unique about Christianity that is not equally satisfied through other religious systems and in short, the world often finds that Christianity is, in and of itself, a pitiful excuse to judge others.

Apostates?

"*Most of us are former Christians, now apostates. Each of us, in our own way, discovered that the Bible is not the word of any god, just a book written by men who wanted to dominate and control others. The priestly caste has always been powerful and influential. We could not find the truth in Christianity and continue to seek elsewhere.*" Comments like these help us understand that at least some folks *do* realize that as far as Christianity is concerned, they *have* apostatized because they have left the faith. Note also their insistence that neither the Bible nor Christianity is true.

Another individual goes into some length, detailing his Christian experience. He states:

"*I used to have a devotional time every morning where I prayed for my friends and family and myself, I read the Bible from cover to cover numerous times during my devotions. I witnessed to my family and they were saved (except my dad, no matter how hard I prayed), I brought up my kids as Christians and led them in the sinners prayer, I spoke in tongues and gave prophecies, I went to prayer meetings and Bible studies, I studied the Bible and prayed with my Christian friends. I **believed** God had a plan for my life, I **believed** he would help me through any situation, I **believed** I had a personal relationship with him. I lived my life for him.*" (emphasis mine)

If anyone were to look at that individual during that time in his life, it would be extremely difficult to say with any surety that he was *not* a Christian. However, *something* happened that caused him and many others to literally turn and walk away from Christianity.

Please note the use of the word "believe" in this person's experience. He stated several times that he *believed* in God, that he *believed* God had a plan for his life, that He would help him in life, etc. He firmly believed these things, yet will now tell you that he *knows* none of it was true.

It is easy to want to say to these folks the usual "Well, if you have fallen away to the point that you now do not believe Christ exists as Mediator and Savior, then you were never a Christian to begin with." The problem with that is that it does not address the situation itself. While it might be correct from the biblical standpoint, it does not explain just exactly what these people turned away *from*, nor does it truly define the Christianity that they believe they were involved in at one time.

My Heart Goes Out
Many, most, or even all of the folks who now say they are ex-Christians are in a unique situation. My heart certainly goes out to them, but beyond that and prayer, nothing can really be done. In fact, these folks would say plainly that they do not *want* you to do anything for them. Leave them alone, they would say. Let them live their lives as they define their lives now. They are happy.

It is difficult to set aside the feelings of sadness for the individual who has "tried" Christ and found Him wanting to the point that they felt there was no recourse but to leave. There is no way that they were in relationship with Him. No way at all.

But What Is the Truth?
In every age, the question of what is actual truth seems to come to the fore. Undoubtedly the most famous exchange between two people where this question arose was between Pilate and Jesus, at His illegal set of trials. We are all too familiar with the fact that for many, truth is relative. For those people, there is no anchor and hence, truth is always changing. However, what is the most difficult aspect of understanding this situation where people have seemingly left the truth of Christ for something else entirely, is hearing how Christianity (and truth itself) is *described* by the ex-Christian.

In other words, when talking with an ex-Christian, he will tell you unambiguously that he *was* in point of fact, a true Christian. Two of these examples have been briefly highlighted, indicating the beliefs held regarding salvation.

If we saw their lives *then,* we would have seen someone who was in every respect, a Christian…*outwardly*. It is difficult to deny that. Since no one can see into the inner life of another, the outward is what we have to go by and our judgment takes place based on what we see.

Do they walk the walk? Do they talk the talk? Do they do what it is believed that Christians do in this world? By their own words, they went to church, they prayed, they helped the poor, they tithed, they read the Bible, and more besides. From every *outward* appearance then, they were Christians.

Yet, these same individuals will just as clearly today state that not only were they *never* Christians, but they now *know* that God does not exist and *never* existed, in the biblical sense.

It cannot be both ways. If God does not exist *now*, because they are atheists, it cannot be that He *did* exist *then* when they fully believed they were Christians. Either God exists from eternity past to eternity future, or He has never existed at all. So the problem is the definition used by the ex-Christian, not the one used by the Christian, and certainly not the one used in the Bible.

The Ex-Marriage
The way the ex-Christian defines being a Christian would be like someone explaining their marriage like this:

Sandy and I were once married. We were married for over 20 years and the marriage was good. We did everything together. We enjoyed our relationship and had many good years with a lot of good times. At some point though, the relationship started to go sour. Not sure why. Could be I got tired, or Sandy got tired, or both. The relationship con-

tinued to go sour to the point that we ultimately realized the only option was divorce.

We have now been divorced for a number of years and life is good. In fact, I have come to the conclusion that I was NEVER actually married to Sandy at all because Sandy does not, nor ever has existed. I know beyond doubt that I was married to Sandy then, but I also now know that Sandy was a sham.

It's good to be free of Sandy, especially since she never existed.

How asinine is that? Who would ever describe a past marriage in that way? Some might want to *forget* the person they were married to and they might want to permanently close and seal that chapter of their life, but to expect others to accept that it never existed is beyond the scope of believability.

More to the point, who would ever *agree* that this could have even *been* a reality? No one would be so gullible. No one would listen to that and respond with, "*Wow, that's interesting. It's great you figured that whole period in your life out, but it's also good that while you were married, you had the companionship of Sandy and some great memories. It's just too bad that you found out she really didn't exist. But since you found out that she did not exist, then there really was nothing left but to seek a divorce. Since you did divorce, then it can be safely and accurately stated that neither Sandy nor the marriage ever existed.*" Right, absolutely, we would all respond with something like that, would we not?

That is just simply absurd. There is no other way to say it. Anyone who told a story like that and expected to be believed would very likely soon be escorted to a rubber room in a nearby psychiatric hospital.

Nevertheless, as intelligent people, we are expected to believe that these folks spent years as *true* Christians, but finally came to the conclusion that it was all a sham. Not only is Christianity *not* true, but for most of them, a personal God does not even exist.

In spite of these disparate views, we are expected to accept as true that an equal amount of believing or knowledge applies to each of their situations.

How does one get from "*I'm a deeply committed Christian*" to the point where they insist with equal vigor "*Not only am I no longer a Christian, but the fact is, God does not even exist!*"? How exactly does that take place?

There are a number of ways this can occur and the process is a fairly simple one. Before going directly there though, it is important to define some more terms related to Christianity.

Is It All Outward?
So what about these ex-Christians? Are they telling the real story? Certainly from their perspective they are, and that cannot, nor should be denied. According to them, they lived it, but now repudiate it. For them, it is as clear as the moon in a cloudless evening sky.

But it must be asked, how does one *know* that they are a Christian to begin with; what are the signs, if there are any signs at all? Can a person truly *know* that Christ lives within them, or is it simply a figment of an overworked imagination? It seems that from everything this author has read, ex-Christians define their lives as Christians based for the most part, on their feelings or actions, not on *faith*. They say they believed, but that is not faith.

The word "Christian" needs to be defined and that will be taken up in the next chapter. First, it would be helpful to define what a Christian is *not*. A true Christian according to the Bible is *not* someone who is one merely outwardly. This is clear from any number of places in the Bible. A true Christian is one who is one inwardly *first* and because of that, the life of Christ is revealed in and through that individual.

Christians become imitators of Christ because His life, through the power of the indwelling Holy Spirit, recreates us into His likeness. By the way, are we ever told that as Christians, we will feel the indwelling presence of the Holy Spirit? No. We are only told that we will see the *outward* manifestation of the Spirit's *indwelling* presence in our lives (I Corinthians 13; Galatians 5:22-23). Since we do not feel His presence, how do we know He is actually there? There is only one way and that is by faith.

What a Christian is Not
To make this clear, we merely need to look at one or two examples from the Bible. In the gospel of John, chapter three, we read a narrative about Nicodemus, a man who was part of a religious group known as the Pharisees. These men were generally highly respected and even feared leaders in the Jewish religious community and came to be so during the time between the Old and New Testaments. This was the period when God chose to turn a deaf ear to the nation of Israel due to their troublesome and consistent failures. It was the equivalent of giving a wayward child a 'timeout.'

The silence during this time was deafening, but it was mercifully lifted at the beginning of John the Baptist's ministry, as he proclaimed the coming of the Messiah. This opens the New Testament for us after roughly 430 years of silence.

Nicodemus – who again, was very religious – sought out Jesus one evening when it would be easy for him to remain in the shadows and out of sight as he spoke with Christ. You see, Nicodemus was taking a huge chance seeking Christ out to begin with, because if word ever got back to his colleagues, things might not go so well for him. He would have had to answer a lot of uncomfortable questions, been made to feel small, called on the carpet, and all the rest.

The Pharisees in general did not like Jesus. He was constantly testing the authority they *thought* they had. They would complain that He regularly put them in embarrassing situations. Jesus for the most part simply responded to their pointed queries in which they tried their best to trap *Him*. They usually attempted this in front of crowds of the everyday individual. It always backfired on them, which was why *they* were often embarrassed. They tried to 'call Him out' only to be broadsided by His wisdom. They wound up eating their words, or looking foolish, or both. Jesus never played their game, but dealt head on with the situation. They complained that Jesus had no respect for their training or position in the community. Their eyes were permanently fixed on Him as they looked and waited for any opportunity to bring this Jesus down. Had they seen one of their own going to Jesus for a Q and A, it would have brought their ire down on their fellow Pharisee as well; in this case, Nicodemus.

As the chapter progresses in the gospel of John, we see that Nicodemus begins the conversation with Jesus in a very respectful way, unlike his Pharisaical comrades. It is difficult to believe though that Nicodemus is quoting other Pharisees at this juncture when he states *"Rabbi, we know that you are a teacher come from God, for no one can do these signs that you do unless God is with him"* John 3:2.

Nicodemus is likely stating what he had heard many of the *common people* say: that Christ was from God. It is clear from Scripture that the Pharisees did not really believe this at all since they were looking for any opportunity to kill Jesus. A person who is respected by a group is not all of a sudden gunned down by that same group. It is simply not a good idea and it goes against the beliefs they hold about that Person (in this case, Christ).

Certainly, God would not like it and He would likely pour out some of His wrath upon anyone who did this. The fact that this was His own Son (*begotten*, or *appointed*, not created) would even create a *greater* infraction of God's law to be sure!

Unfortunately the Pharisees, unable to see that Jesus was the Messiah sent from God to Israel, thought instead that He was a blasphemer. Because of that, He deserved death according to the Mosaic Law. Not *once* did it occur to these religious bigots that He could have in fact, been the Messiah. It is interesting to hear people today say that Jesus was a good man, a good teacher, but not God. It is also interesting to hear these same people say the religious leaders misunderstood Jesus. When He spoke in parables, yes, because they were blind to the truth those parables taught. But when He made statements like "Before Abraham was, I AM," they knew *exactly* what He was saying. They were far from being idiots. They did *not* misunderstand Him.

If Jesus was not trying to say that He was in fact God, it would have been brainless of Him to use terminology that they would have taken to identify Him as God. Because He purposefully incited the religious leaders by using terms that pointed back to Him as God is the strongest indication that He was in fact, either God the Son, or a complete moron. Enough of this nonsense that "Jesus was a good man and a good teacher, but not God."

Jesus' response to Nicodemus is quite significant. It received an immediate reaction from Nicodemus. His reaction is probably how most of us would have reacted as well. Jesus said *"Truly, truly, I say to you, unless one is born again he cannot see the kingdom of God."* (John 3:3)

It is not difficult to imagine Nicodemus' thoughts at this point, which were probably something like "*Huh? What was that Jesus? I have to be...what?*" However, what he actually said was "*How can a man be born when he is old? Can he enter a second time into his mother's womb and be born?*" (John 3:4)

It Is Not Outward
Please note that Jesus is clearly stating a truth of ultimate spiritual proportions here. He is telling Nicodemus plainly that he needs a

new birth. This is *not* an outward exercise of the Christian life, or even a set of mental exercises, or head knowledge. It is nothing less than an inward reality created solely by the Holy Spirit, which generates an *outward* expression. That inner reality produces a change of character within the individual and replaces old desires with new desires that now glorify the Lord.

It is this *spiritual transaction* which gives rise to an inner and then an outer transformation. What we used to do, we begin to no longer *want* to do. The way we used to talk, we no longer want to talk. We begin to want to do things that please God and because of the new birth, we now have that *ability within* to do that. Jesus is very clearly indicating that without this new birth (spiritual transaction), there is <u>no</u> salvation.

This new birth that Christ spoke of is extremely important for any number of reasons. Chief among them is the implication that Nicodemus was very likely already *doing* the things that most of us would agree are things that make a Christian *look* like a Christian. He was undoubtedly caring for the poor, reading and studying Scripture, praying, singing hymns, worshipping, and all the rest that went along with being a Pharisee.

But please take note: *nowhere* does Jesus say to Nicodemus that he must devote himself to *more* prayer, to *more* alms, to *more* good deeds, or to anything else. Christ knew that he was already doing those things, but that doing those things *does not a Christian make*, and certainly did not provide eternal life.

Had that been the case, nothing else would have been needed by Nicodemus and certainly Christ would not have needed to die. What Nicodemus *did* need was a *second birth*. Can you imagine how Nicodemus felt? If your heart does not go out to this man, you have no feeling. He was bewildered. He did not understand what Jesus was saying, even though they were both speaking the same language.

In response to Nicodemus' puzzlement, Jesus said *"Truly, truly, I say to you, unless one is born of water and the Spirit, he cannot enter the kingdom of God. That which is born of the flesh is flesh, and that which is born of the Spirit is spirit. Do not marvel that I said to you, 'You must be born again.' The wind blows where it wishes, and you hear its sound, but you do not know where it comes from or where it goes. So it is with everyone who is born of the Spirit."* (John 3:5-8)

Nicodemus was likely inwardly sighing at this point, because what Jesus just said did not clarify things for him. In fact, it made it more confusing. This is apparent from his response of *"How can these things be?"* (John 3:9).

Jesus was speaking plainly, telling Nicodemus that he had already been born once (*born of flesh*), but He needed to be born again (*born of the Spirit*). Jesus might just as well have been speaking English or Spanish to our friend Nicodemus for all the understanding he managed to get out of that conversation. He was still scratching his head about how to enter his mother's womb a second time, and had not moved on from there.

Before letting him off the hook, Jesus asked him *"Are you the teacher of Israel and yet you do not understand these things?"* John 3:10. Ouch. That must have hurt a bit, but Jesus was not trying to hurt him. He was merely trying to help him see that even with all of his training as a Pharisee, he had gotten no closer to grasping God's perspective on eternal life, and that was sadly unfortunate. It is obvious though that Jesus loved him because He took the time to talk with Nicodemus and His patience toward him is evident.

Prophetic Insight
Jesus continues to explain to Nicodemus what He means, providing Nicodemus with a bit of prophetic insight by telling him how He (Jesus) would be lifted up just as the bronze serpent was lifted up by Moses in the Old Testament. This would allow anyone who believed

in Him to receive eternal life, as the ancient Israelites did when they looked upon the bronze serpent after they had been bitten by a real poisonous snake. This entire conversation leads up to what is undoubtedly the most famous verse in all of Scripture, John 3:16, which says *"For God so loved the world, that he gave his only Son, that whoever believes in him should not perish but have eternal life."*

The entire point here is that in order to become a Christian, there must be a new birth; a *spiritual transaction*. It is not enough to say that one is a Christian because of all the things they may have *done*, or even because of the things they have *believed*, including a particular "story of Christianity." Many people do that, yet they are not Christians. They can do all the good works they wish to do. They can pray until they are blue in the face, or run out of breath entirely. They can believe with all their heart that they truly are Christian, but when all is said and done, they are not Christians **IF** the required spiritual transaction has never taken place. Only God definitively knows whether or not this transaction has occurred within each individual. He alone judges the hearts of men.

Christianity Practically Speaking
As an aside, this transformation that takes place within each true Christian takes the remainder of his earthly life to work itself out. While the new birth takes place in an instant of time, the *process* of being recreated into Christ's image stretches over the remaining years of that person's life. It is no different than physical birth. The baby is born at an exact moment in time, but takes an entire lifetime to grow and mature. This is Christianity, practically speaking.

Some individuals see tremendous change occurring within almost immediately. Others find that this change is more subtle; not so noticeable. It is the difference between the rushing of water over a broken dam, and a small stream of water consistently carrying the runoff from a greater body of water to another place. In both cases the change does occur, but the amount of change and the speed of the change varies from Christian to Christian.

If a Christian can look back over his life after twenty or thirty years and see essentially no progress at all, it becomes an excellent time to ask if that spiritual transaction ever truly happened in the first place. Was the commitment to Christ and the resultant "regeneration" by Him only outward? In other words, does the Christian sense that everything done for Christ is done from the outside, with no discernable change that becomes a motivation from within? Does love for others (especially other Christians) exist from *within* or is it something that is done because it is supposed to be done? Does your nature fight against it, or does it seem natural to love and forgive people, unlike what it might have been like previously?

Is there a real sense of joy of knowing that salvation has been granted? Have the desires that used to be worldly and enjoyable in that realm been replaced with desires that now have eternal value? If no noticeably real and lasting change is seen, there is an excellent chance that person's life is devoid of true Christianity. How do we know this? Because the Bible is replete with promises God has made to His children regarding the growth that will take place in their lives; I Corinthians 13 and Galatians 5 are just two of them. The Psalms are filled with these promises. If they are not taking place in a person's life, it is likely not the fault of God.

There are many people who will stand before Christ one day, only to be ultimately rejected by Him. These people will say things like "But Lord, didn't I do this in your Name and didn't I do this other thing?" These *outward* actions unfortunately, did not stem from an *inner* transformation. Because of this, they will be rejected by Christ simply because He did not *know* them; they had no *relationship* with Him. That is actually wonderful. Think about it. A person's salvation is not dependent upon what they did in this life, but is dependent upon whether or not they were actually in relationship to Him. Entering into a relationship with Jesus occurs the moment that spiritual transactions takes place.

Matthew 7
In this chapter, starting in verse twenty-one, the Lord describes the scene in which people are being judged. It seems to be an abbreviated form of the longer parable of the Sheep and the Goats found in chapter twenty-five of Matthew.

Notice that many who will stand before Christ in judgment, will point to what they did in this life, saying they " *'prophes[ied] in your name and cast out demons in your name, and (did) many mighty works in your name'.* " The Lord's response is but a simple "*I never knew you. Depart from me...*" (Matthew 7:22-23)

There are many alive today (pastors, evangelists, faith healers, 'good' people, morally upright people, teachers, and many others), who will stand before Christ on the day of judgment, convinced that what they accomplished in this life has given them eternal life in the next. This is simply not the case though. At least some of these to be sure, knew themselves to be fakes because this is the way they lived their lives here; as fakes, or charlatans. But then you have the other group which the Bible classifies as *professing* Christians. These folks may actually get to the point of believing themselves to be Christians because they see no difference between the way they lived their life compared to those who are true Christians. It will be in that knowledge they will die and find themselves standing before God.

Jesus' use of the words "*I never knew you...*" is very important. Notice those who are rejected point to the many things they have done in Christ's Name. They believe their good works should outweigh any 'bad' they produced in their life. Their thinking is deluded though. They are 'bad' *because* of the sin nature within them, even if they had done nothing specifically 'bad' in this life (which is impossible *since* the sin nature is inherent within each individual). So it stands to reason that even their 'good' works are not really good, by God's standards.

This belief they hold about themselves fails to see the point, which is clearly brought out by Christ in His condemnation of them. He states that He never *knew* them. This is quite a bit different than saying, "Your works were not good enough." This does not even enter the picture. Get that if nothing else.

Salvation is based on a *relationship* with Jesus that *begins* with the new birth; the spiritual transaction we have discussed. Salvation is *not* based on works that a person does. Actual works that God considers to be good, *flow* from a transformed inner life, bringing glory to God, not the person.

The new birth is the *beginning* of the eternal life and the Christian's walk with God. That life from then on will continue to grow in Christ, as His character is recreated in the Christian, ultimately making each Christian fit for eternity. Without that new birth there is *no* eternal life, because there is no relationship with the Eternal God.

Good works just do not cut it. Walking the walk and talking the talk do not make a Christian. The new birth *causes* inner *then* outer lasting change. The Holy Spirit does the work. The Christian cooperates by being willing to allow that to happen.

Not a Christian
This is why true Christians say that the ex-Christians were never really Christians to begin with. The ex-Christians had no real relationship with Jesus, therefore they were *never* Christians. The ex-Christians define Christianity as something that it is *not,* and then get upset with the Christians because they appear to be condemning the ex-Christians. This is not the case. The Christians are not condemning the ex-Christians. The ex-Christians have already condemned themselves. The true Christians are simply *clarifying* the situation by

pointing out the definition of being a Christian, as revealed in Scripture.

The ex-Christians on the other hand, are attaching an incorrect definition to what it means to be a Christian and then getting upset that true Christians do not like their definition. The reality though, is that the ex-Christians are completely off the mark when it comes to their definition of what it means to be a Christian, and because of that, they *should* be corrected, whether they like it or not.

Fred, the Psychiatrist
By way of example, it would be possible to dress up in an expensive suit, drive a pricey car and head to an expensive office suite every day. It would further be possible to have that office filled with books on psychology and actual cases of clients that dealt with psychiatry. Beyond this, there could be an administrative assistant or secretary just beyond the office door. A business card could have all the normal information on it related to being a psychiatrist. People would come to the office expecting to be helped through a difficult time in their life.

Invoices would be sent to clients indicating that services are $300 per hour. Luncheons might be attended where other psychiatrists routinely attend and get to know one another.

Hours, nights and weekends might be spent pouring over psychiatric notes and transcripts from other cases that are similar to the one currently involved in. Other psychiatrists might be called, asking their opinion on a matter.

From every outward appearance, I am a psychiatrist. I act like one. I talk like one. I send out bills like one. There is nothing to indicate that I am not a real psychiatrist. After a while, I might even come to the point of believing my own press. After all, the only thing that separates me from being a real psychiatrist is the lack of a degree and a license from the state. I took care of that though by having fake ones made up. As far as everyone else is concerned, I am a psychiatrist and I have clients to prove it.

Whether a police officer, a doctor, a lawyer, a psychiatrist, an evangelist, or minister, or something else entirely, people have pretended to be something they are not for centuries. The only thing that has stopped them normally is either getting caught, or dying; one or the other.

In point of fact though, I am *not*, nor have I ever been a real psychiatrist, and I have certainly never pretended to be one to take people's money. The closest I have come to being a real psychiatrist was when I acted as one for a film project. I was told I was very convincing on camera and it was a lot of fun, but that was the extent of my foray into the field of psychiatry.

No matter how real I appeared on camera, I was not a real psychiatrist because the actual *transaction* never took place. I had never gone to graduate school for that degree, nor had I ever taken or passed the required state exams in order to obtain a state license to open a practice. Yet here I was, being a psychiatrist, acting like a psychiatrist and for all intents and purposes, I was a psychiatrist...on film.

This little story merely serves to point out that just because someone says or even believes they are a Christian, it does not necessarily mean that they *are* a Christian. The story is also *not* an attempt to insinuate that ex-Christians are being purposefully duplicitous when claiming to be real Christians. In fact it is very likely that most firmly believed themselves to *be* actual Christians. The point of the brief story about the psychiatrist serves simply to show that outward appearances are not always based on inner reality.

De-Conversions
To read some of the de-conversion testimonials written by those who

left Christianity is to underscore some commonalities which exist between all of them.

One individual says this about the Christian experience:

"For over a year now I've been seeking God through a faithful Christian walk- mostly independent of church membership because I didn't want to become "religious" and nowhere in the Bible does it say to join a church. So, I occasionally went to church services- always at different ones- but almost always left disappointed and confused. Every church I attended had merchandise for sale and forcefully asked for money to build a new gym or something.

"I wanted to go to church to worship and praise God- not shop or buy my salvation. Many people in the church keep pure hearted people out. Many times I was either watched and chastised after or even during the service for sitting too comfortably or was completely ignored. Anyway, I found myself being instructed to do this and that- formulas to healing and salvation."

The problem is obvious. This person's concept of being a faithful Christian is false. First, he believed he could have a faithful walk with God apart from church. He believed that the Bible does not teach that you have to join a church. But Paul, in his letter to the Corinthians, makes it clear that people should attend services *regularly*. Fellowship and growth happen within the context of being with other members of the Body of Christ. It cannot happen in a vacuum unless God has specifically set you aside as He did with John the Baptist.

Regarding the problem of these churches wanting money all the time, the person should keep looking until the right church is found, and granted sometimes that can take a while.

Another individual says it this way, regarding rejecting Christianity:

"I guess the best thing to compare religion to, in general, is the movie, The Matrix, because if you are convinced that something is real, and you believe it, how could it be false, just like the whole web of lies involved in the biggest cult movement ever."

So to this person, the Matrix makes sense, therefore that is probably what is happening behind the scenes for Christians, who create their own fake reality by believing in Christ, etc.

Still another individual makes these comments about God and the Bible:

"How...did Moses know what went on before the flood - or even at the time of the patriarchs? I don't think that God dictated the book of Genesis to him. Especially with the differing accounts of Creation which just _don't_ resolve properly. Particularly the bit where vegetation gets created before the sun does. Quite clearly Moses collected the folk stories of the Jewish people and attempted to wring some coherent sense out of them. If not for the fact that Christianity, to make any sense, requires original sin which requires an original Adam and Eve, I could happily have dismissed the garden of Eden story as the legend it quite obviously is. Talking snakes indeed."

Whether this person realizes it or not, he has contradicted himself a number of times in his statement. The second to last sentence is unclear. The writer seems to be saying that it is because of Christianity that he believes the Adam and Eve story. Otherwise he would have tossed the whole line of thinking.

This person seems also confused about the order of creation and the syntax of the text itself. Because of the syntax, it is very likely that the sun and moon and stars were created in *verse three*, but were not fully separated until after vegetation was created. Since light (day) was created in verse three of Genesis one, the result is the first morning and evening occurring in verse five; a twenty-four hour period.

There was obviously already enough light available for plants and vegetation to grow.

It is not all that different when comparing Genesis chapters one and two. In chapter one, Moses provides an overall account of the Creation, whereas in chapter two, he goes *back* and includes more detail about the creation of Adam and Eve. No biggie there.

It is apparent that this individual's view of God is rather small. The second sentence in which it is stated "*I don't think that God dictated the book of Genesis to him*" is ironic, because that is probably exactly how it *was* done. But why would someone simply come to that conclusion and what is it based on? Where is the empirical data to support his conclusion?

The next sentence regarding all the different accounts of creation not matching up is easy to explain.

According to the Bible, the flood took place in Genesis 6 and ended in Genesis 9. By chapter 11 of Genesis, a great deal of time had gone by because the world had repopulated itself. The text also states that people spoke only one language. Knowing that the people would band together and stop at nothing to accomplish their own selfish goals, God chose to confuse them by creating different languages and cultures. He also wanted them to disperse and populate the entire globe, not merely one section of it, and as long as they spoke the same language, there would be no real reason for them to move away from one another. After God made this change, people began to migrate to other areas of the world with those who spoke the same language as they did.

Keeping Track of History
Oral records of past history were undoubtedly passed down as told by Noah to his sons, and to their sons, and to their sons, etc. Since archaeology has indicated that almost all ancient civilizations have

some form of the account of a global flood (with names changed, etc.) it stands to reason that these groups of people, now scattered by God with new languages, adopted new names for Noah and the Noahic events. This then would account for discrepancies.

Regarding God using Moses to get the Creation account correct, He likely did dictate to Moses, or told Moses the story allowing Moses to put things down in his own thoughts. God had obviously dictated a great deal to Moses during the Exodus, especially on Mt. Sinai. It is difficult to know why something like this would be hard to believe…unless one's view of God is exceedingly small. But the individual simply makes a statement that he assumes to be fact, yet does nothing to back it up. From looking elsewhere in the Bible though, we can determine that there were times when God dictated directly to Moses. This makes it simple to accept the fact that God likely did the same when it came time for Moses to write the Creation account.

This individual also concludes that the Creation account is myth, but he offers no substantial proof to support his claim. He simply decided that it is myth. Where is the scientific process? Where is the empirical data?

Another ex-Christian writes:

"Also why would an unconditionally loving God have hell [be] an ETERNAL hell?"

Eternal Punishment
The problem of hell is certainly not an easy topic to deal with, but it is important to note that Jesus talked more about hell than any other subject. There are a number of reasons why hell is eternal. The largest reason has to do with the fact that just because people die and go into eternity, it does not mean that they stop *sinning*. They will continue to sin forever (because they have died in their sin, with their sin nature intact, which controls what they do, say and think in the

here and now). It will control what they do, say and think in the hereafter as well. That stands to reason.

Just as importantly (or possibly more so), sin is absolutely and completely reprehensible to God. It is abhorrent. We do not realize just how repulsive sin truly is at its root. In fact, we often compare ourselves to others and determine we are 'not that bad.'

The problem of course is that when we are judged, we will be judged against the righteousness of Christ and His alone. He is *the* standard by which all are judged and no one will get even close to that standard. This is why salvation exchanges our *unrighteousness* for His *righteousness*. A Christian stands before God and is judged based on Christ's imputed righteousness. God looks at us and sees Christ's righteousness, not ours. Because He sees Christ's righteousness, it is also understood that the individual is in relationship with Jesus Christ, the Eternal Son of God.

The Bible states that sin is lawlessness and God is a God of law, order and structure. Just one sin breaks that order and God must destroy it. Those who choose to remain chained to their sin by rejecting salvation through Christ as they go from this life to the next, are destroyed with it. Being destroyed biblically *never* means annihilated.

Without Faith...
We could go on with many other testimonies of those who have departed from the faith, but the truth can be seen. The biggest snare for the person who moves away from Christianity, is found in his inability to persevere in the faith. This usually stems from the fact that he often winds up judging situations by his feelings, instead of by God's Word.

The truly sad part of all these so-called testimonials is that each of these individuals has essentially become their own highest authority in life, especially in spiritual things.

They have found reasons why they are no longer involved in Christianity, however they have based those reasons solely on how they often *feel* about certain things.

It does not make sense *to them* that God would allow people to choose to be remanded to hell for all eternity, so they reject it. They do not *believe* that God might have dictated Genesis to Moses, so they reject it. If believing that there was a "first" man in Adam and a "first" woman in Eve is too difficult for them, it is rejected.

Who Needs the Bible Anyway?
In spite of any and all external (or even internal) evidence that proves much of the biblical record, with the Bible itself providing a great deal of useful and accurate information about many past civilizations and even scientific principles, it is cast off because it appears to them to be more like a fairy tale than anything factual.

They have become their own supreme authority; their own god. Their eyes are now open, as the Serpent said they would be, by rejecting God's authority and rule.

Unfortunately for them, if Christianity is true, they will not be answering to themselves in the end, but to God who is no respecter of persons and judges fairly.

Chapter 2

As indicated in the previous chapter, the true Christian is one because of a *spiritual transaction* that has taken place within. This was made patently clear in the narrative involving the conversation between Nicodemus and Jesus, in John chapter three.

Webster's Dictionary defines a Christian as "*a person professing belief in Jesus as the Christ or in the religion based on the teaching of Jesus.*" From the standpoint of the world, that works, but in reality, it does not go far enough. Based on that, we can see why ex-Christians can claim that they were once Christians. This definition may serve as a starting point, but more needs to be added because there is no biblical application in Webster's definition. Certainly the best place to find the definition of a Christian is in the Bible itself.

In the New Testament, the word "Christian" is used three times: twice in Acts and once in 1 Peter (Acts 11:26; Acts 26:28; 1 Peter 4:16). Acts informs us that believers were first referred to as Christians in the city of Antioch. It was because they were imitating Christ in the way they lived. This was not necessarily a compliment though, but a sign of contempt, since Christ was hated and a good deal of persecution existed.

Today someone is thought to be a Christian if they are Mormon, or highly religious, or moral, or simply because they attend church, or because they speak out against immorality, or they crusade against vices of society, or even if they own or carry a Bible. None of these serve to explain what a true Christian is though. In the case of the Mormon, the doctrine between Christianity and Mormonism is so far removed there are virtually no commonalities between the two.

Church Goers
People who go to church often refer to themselves as Christian, yet this cannot be so because going to church is simply another outward sign, which anyone can do. That by itself does not confirm that the person is a true Christian.

Nicodemus had spent his adult life doing things, including good works as part of his religious duty, however it was not good enough as Christ informed him. Good works does not a Christian make. Throughout the New Testament, it should become clear that our good works amount to nothing. Ultimately, a true Christian is one who is "born again." Peter refers to this as well in I Peter 1:23, telling his readers *"since you have been born again, not of perishable seed but of imperishable, through the living and abiding word of God."* Being born again results in a saving faith in Christ, who becomes the object of our faith and trust. The relationship that begins with him then is eternal in nature.

Real Christians
A true Christian then, is someone who loves God above all things and loves others, especially those of the faith (1 John 2:4; 1 John 2:10), from a *pure* motivation. This reality occurs *because* of the new life within. This pure love is the main evidence of the new birth that has taken place within, and the eternal relationship with Jesus that has begun.

When people attempt to love others and do the things that they *believe* are the things Christians should do, they wind up doing those things either from a wrong motivation, by using their own energy, or both. Isaiah 64:6 tells us *"We have all become like one who is unclean, and all our righteous deeds are like a polluted garment."*

No matter how wonderful things may appear on the outside, if God views our attempts at righteousness as "filthy rags" then it is obvious that something needs to change *within us*. That something is only found in the new life which takes root within us. This comes from a realization of our utter inability to please God in any way, shape or form, using our own strength. Our 'good works' do not cut it for God. They are all filthy, disgusting rags of human effort, lacking the purity God requires.

Another individual describes his Christian conversion this way: *"My personal journey of de-conversion can be viewed in a similar light as a story of an addict. One day you feel great and have no fear of hell and the need to tell others about it, but the other day you wake up and feel like Christ is real, what you have experienced is true, and Christianity is the way."*

That comment is also ambiguous. It really does not zero in on how or why he felt that Christianity was no longer true, or how he would define being a Christian in the first place.

More De-Conversions

Another individual who is becoming well known in the ex-Christian circles has written a book about himself and his life, both as a Christian pastor and now as an ex-Christian. One advertising blurb for his book reads this way, *"Looking for a good introduction to atheism without all the technical philosophical jargon? Barker's book is for you! As a former minister turned atheist, Dan Barker documents the arguments that "deconverted" him from Christian fundamentalist to atheist. Losing Faith in Faith is an arsenal for skeptics and a challenge to believers."*[1]

In fact, there are any number of books available today extolling the virtues of atheism and the multitude of reasons for leaving Christianity in the dust. The authors of these books offer a cold, hard look at their actual experiences, as they traveled the path *as* Christians and then *away* from it altogether into atheism.

The Internet is also filled with testimonies from individuals who have either exchanged their faith in Christ for an alternative gospel, or have come to believe that there is no God at all. Titles of testimonies like:

- From Christian to Atheist
- From Good Catholic boy to Heretic Atheist
- My "De-conversion" Story

---

[1] http://secweb.infidels.org/?kiosk=books&id=41

- Dare to Think for Yourself: A Journey from Faith to Reason
- Losing My Religion: Why I Left Christianity
- The Journey Out
- Becoming an Atheist

...and so on.

What do all these people have in common? They firmly *believe* that at one point they were in fact Christians. They then came to another point in their life which caused them to just as firmly believe that Christianity was a sham, a con, and had not one iota of truth in it, except for the fact that maybe Jesus Christ actually lived on this planet at one point.

Being a Christian means much more than just *doing things* (or even having head knowledge about something). Becoming a Christian means that a spiritual transaction or new birth has taken place within the individual. It sounds more and more, based on this definition, that those who call themselves ex-Christians were Christians in *name* only. How could it be otherwise? They would have to agree with that because if, as they say, there is no God, then there was no God with whom to have a spiritual transaction or new birth.

Again, this is certainly something that these ex-Christian folks do not like to hear, but that matters little. We cannot go by their definition of what being a Christian means. We must go by the Bible's definition of what it means to be a Christian.

Are there any other examples that provide us with a biblical view of being a Christian? Not only are there other examples, but the writers of the New Testament have a great deal to say on the subject as well.

The Woman at the Well
This particular situation from the gospel of John is enlightening due to what it reveals about Christianity and its Founder, Jesus Christ. This is also an interesting situation because the woman Jesus was

speaking with here was a Samaritan. In Jesus' day, folks from Samaria were looked down upon by Jews as being uncouth and unclean. Jews did not associate with them unless they had to do so.

Based on that alone, we can understand the surprise of the woman as we read the narrative in the gospel of John, chapter four, verses one through forty-two. Jesus had left Judea for Galilee. On His way, He had to pass through Samaria and wound up stopping in a small village named Sychar. You may remember Sychar from the Old Testament because this is the area in which Jacob gave his son Joseph a field. The well that Joseph used as a boy was still there in Christ's time, and people still drew water from it.

Jesus stopped to rest near the well. As He did, a woman came by to draw water for herself. Jesus took this opportunity to ask for a drink from her. This of course was not only extremely unusual, but something an orthodox Jew would not have done due to the fact that it might cause him to become ceremonially unclean. This in turn, would require a week of ritual cleansing before he would be able to step into the Temple again. Jesus did not appear to be concerned about being "unclean."

The woman was surprised as well, asking in John 4:9, "*How is it that you, a Jew, ask for a drink from me, a woman of Samaria?*" Jesus was not alarmed at the fact that He had spoken to this woman, responding to her in verse 10 with, "*If you knew the gift of God, and who it is that is saying to you, 'Give me a drink,' you would have asked him, and he would have given you living water.*" So what was Jesus saying here? First of all, He was piquing her interest. She was certainly interested because she replied with, "*Sir, you have nothing to draw water with, and the well is deep. Where do you get that living water? Are you greater than our father Jacob? He gave us the well and drank from it himself, as did his sons and his livestock*" (John 4:11-12).

This is the same type of conversation that Jesus had with Nicodemus. Jesus is saying one thing, but understood to be saying something else entirely. He goes on in the second part of verse fourteen to offer her water that will literally quench her thirst forever: *"The water that I will give him will become in him a spring of water welling up to eternal life."*

The phrase "eternal life" got her attention. She knew what that meant and she was very interested, though she may not have completely understood what Jesus was saying. This is evidenced by her response in verse fifteen: *"The woman said to him, 'Sir, give me this water, so that I will not be thirsty or have to come here to draw water.'"*

Interestingly enough, Jesus changes the subject a bit here and tells her to go and get her husband. Why? For several reasons. The husband was (and is) the head of the home. He is responsible for the spiritual as well as physical welfare of his wife and children. He is not to be a tyrant or dictator, but is to love them as Christ loves His Church. Jesus also knew that she did not have a husband and was giving her an opportunity to either admit or deny that fact.

The woman truthfully confessed to Jesus that she did not have a husband. Because of her honesty, Jesus revealed his deity by letting her know that He knew she did not have a husband. Moreover, He pointed out to her that she had five previous husbands and the one she was now living with was also not her husband.

Would this not shock anyone? How could a complete stranger know intimate things about a person He had never met? Only God would be capable of that. Jesus tells her in verse twenty-six that He is the awaited Messiah.

At this point, His disciples returned. Seeing that Jesus was talking to this Samaritan woman shocked them a bit (the English Standard Version states "marveled"), but no one dared ask Him about it. They figured He must have known who she was and what He was doing, so they left it unasked, but still wondered.

The Exchanged Life in Christ
So what is the point to this narrative? The point is that in both situations with Nicodemus and this Samaritan woman, Christ introduced them to a new concept; a concept that they had not heard about.

For Nicodemus, he had to be born again. For this Samaritan woman, she needed living water that produced eternal life. Both concepts pointed to the same thing; a *spiritual rebirth* or *transaction* was required. An exchange takes place with the sinner's *unrighteousness*, replaced with Christ's *perfect righteousness*.

Obviously in both cases, Christ uses figurative language to illustrate their need. In both cases, Jesus highlights the fact that something *internal* was necessary in order to receive salvation (eternal life). In *neither* case does Jesus focus on the outward by urging them to greater works. He completely bypasses that, directing their attention instead to what goes on *inside* a person, in their spirit.

So the question for the ex-Christian then is whether or not they in fact, had this spiritual transaction take place inwardly. From everything read so far – their testimonials, their de-conversions, their reasons for leaving Christianity to begin with – all of it boils down to how they perceive their *experience*. They have relied on how they *felt* regarding their Christianity.

In nearly all cases, the emphasis (by them) has been on what their feelings have told them about Christ, the Bible, Christianity, Christians, etc. In fact, many testimonials speak of being "burned" by Christians, or the pastor, or the church in general. The focus is on *them* – their feelings - and how Christianity has supposedly dealt with *them*. It was a full set of circumstances like these that have in most cases, caused them to turn away, leaving the faith entirely, and ultimately for most, adopting an atheistic view of life. But it is clear that their entire outlook was centered on themselves, even as Christians!

Should this situation be *odd* to us? Should we begin to question the validity of Christ and Christianity? Should we begin to crumble under the weight of this mountain of people who have left the faith? Is God somehow unfaithful? Has He deliberately pulled the plug on these folks? Worse yet, does He *not* exist?

These are good, necessary questions; questions that deserve answers and fortunately for us, the Bible has them. Now, if the reader is one who does not view the Bible as the Supreme Authority in all matters related to faith and practice, then the author would encourage you to plow through this next chapter to at least hear how the Bible responds to those who seemingly walk away from the faith.

Chapter 3

When a farmer plants a crop, he certainly hopes to have a harvest. It is that harvest which allows him to plant crops for next year, and take care of his livestock and family now. Ask any farmer and they will tell you that it takes a certain type of soil to grow a successful crop that in turn, becomes a successful harvest. Weather is also part of the picture, allowing the crops to grow well, but without the right kind of soil conditions, there is little point to planting crops at all.

Because most of the people during Jesus' time were either farmers (or gardeners), or fishermen, they knew a great deal about crops, planting seed, weather patterns, and the harvest. Since this was their experience, Jesus spoke to them using illustrations that would capture their attention in ways they would understand.

The Sower
A well known parable from the gospels of Matthew, Mark and Luke relates the experiences of a person who sows (or plants) seed. This parable was taught on a day when Jesus left the house where He was staying and went to sit down at the edge of the sea.

Because of who Jesus was and the renown that surrounded Him, it was not long before the crowds found Him and gathered around to see what He might teach them that day.

In order to be heard, Matthew 13:3 tells us that "*He got into a boat and sat down, and the whole crowd was standing on the beach.*" Jesus got into a boat, and likely let it drift off shore a bit in order that the water would act as a bounce board for His voice. Since there were no microphones and speaker systems then, it became necessary to use the things in nature for an advantage when speaking to an outdoor crowd. So it was that Jesus, knowing His voice would literally bounce off the surface of the water, allowing even those in the back of the crowd to hear what He had to say, told the parable.

So what does He tell them? He speaks of a man who sows seed. Some of the seed fell on areas beside the road. Other seed was grabbed and eaten by birds. More of the seed fell on rocky places, where little nourishing soil existed. Still other seed fell among thorns, but finally some of the seed fell on good soil, allowing the seed to germinate, grow and produce a harvest (cf. 13:1-9). You have to appreciate how Jesus ends many of His parables with the words "He who has an ear, let him hear" (v. 10). He is literally calling them to seek to understand the parable.

At this point, the disciples asked Him why He taught the people in parables; why not simply speak plainly? Jesus told them that it was for them (the disciples) to know the meaning of the parables (or the *mysteries of heaven*, as in the ESV), but to the general public it had not been granted. He then refers to passages in Isaiah which speak of the people who always hear, but never understand, who always see, but do not perceive (cf. Isaiah 6:9). God's sovereignty always oversees all situations. He will open the ears of those whom He will open, otherwise their ears will remain in their natural condition: *closed*. Who will question Him on that?

The Explanation
Jesus confides in His disciples, explaining to them the meaning of the Parable of the Sower. According to Matthew 13:18-23, the seed sown by the roadside represents seed that has been sown, but is *unable* to take root. Some of it is taken and eaten by birds - which represent Satan and his demonic cohorts - before it can even begin to take root.

The seed that is sown on rocky places represents the person who hears the good news of salvation and rejoices, resulting in an emotionally based reaction, which is not necessarily wrong in and of itself. The good news *should* bring joy. However, because the seed is unable to establish a good, solid root, it is only temporary. Once the difficulties through persecution from the world gain a foothold in his life, his joy vanishes and he falls away (cf. v. 21). Does this sound like many who refer to themselves as ex-Christian? It could very well be the case.

The seed sown among the thorns represents worrying about ways to acquire as much wealth as possible and keeping it once it is gotten. It is easy to see how those two go together. A person worries about ways to become wealthy, and once they begin to acquire that wealth, they worry about ways not only to keep it, but to obtain more. Because of this, any seed sown in that person's heart becomes "unfruitful" (cf. v. 22). It is impossible to serve God and money at the same time.

The good soil of course represents the seed sown in the one who "hears and understands it." There are roughly eighteen Greek words that were used in the Bible to signify "understanding." The Greek word used in this particular instance for "understands" is *syniēmi*. *"The dominant sense is that of rational and spiritual comprehension, or discernment, of the word of God and the gospel. Syniēmi refers to people 'being granted insight' into God's word, the truth of the gospel."*[2]

Understanding here means a deep, abiding knowledge which leads to action. It is not simply head knowledge. It is almost like being enlightened about something. The person in this parable who bears fruit through witnessing or evangelizing, and serves the Lord with all his heart (cf. v. 23), does so because of his understanding or perception about something.

Notice this person did not necessarily have a huge emotional reaction. While he undoubtedly appreciated and was awed by God's love for him, that appreciation translated to the outward expression of that, which was evangelizing and witnessing. He was completely dedicated to His purposes. His main goal was to see souls *saved*.

Looking back over the parable, it is painfully clear that even though the seed is sown among different types of soil, only *one type* actually succeeds in bearing fruit which ultimately leads to eternal life.

---

[2] Stephen D. Renn, Ed., *Expository Dictionary of Bible Words* (Peabody: Henrickson Publishers 2005), 1001

There are four different types of soils represented in the parable, yet only one type is able to hear *and* understand it, allowing it to take deep root, bearing a good deal of fruit. Is it any wonder that Jesus tells us that few will find the narrow path that leads to eternal life and that we should literally "struggle" to find it? (Matthew 7:14)

In this parable, it is obvious that some *believe* they are Christians, yet wind up walking away for one reason or another. People have long debated the doctrine of *"once saved, always saved,"* vs. *"saved, but able to reject."* But if a person is truly saved, are they able to reject Christ?

Suffice it to say that in these parables, people *do* walk away from the faith. It is this author's belief that only one situation (the good soil) represents a true Christian. Note that Jesus indicates that it is only the "good soil" that receives and *understands* the seed (gospel). Jesus points out the fact that the gospel is not based on emotionalism, or simply head knowledge, but an understanding that changes that individual's life permanently because it literally wells up from within.

This does not preclude an individual from *understanding* the good news of Jesus Christ and *reacting* to it with joy, thinking "Wow, that's awesome!" There could in fact be a great deal of joy for the sinner who realizes what Christ has done for him.

What Jesus appears to be saying though, is that our emotions alone do not *create* that comprehension, but they merely *react* to it. It does no good to be joyful over something that is not understood well. As soon as the joy is gone (either pushed out by circumstances, or through a lack of understanding), a sense of frustration and/or confusion can then take its place.

Confusion born of frustration may cause one to throw up his hands and say "Forget it! I'll run my own life!" This may take some time to get to, after he first hears and "believes" the gospel.

The individual begins to firmly believe he was duped into believing something that did not, nor does exist. The next steps involve turning away from the faith, and becoming the captain of his own life and fate. This line of thinking is nothing new. It is the same thinking that took place in the Garden of Eden, with Adam and Eve questioning not only God's authority, but the true meaning behind what He had actually stated to them ("Did God really say...?).

Adam's and Eve's ultimate rejection of God's law resulted from their answers to the questions 1) why would God not want us to become like Him, and 2) why would God really not want us to eat the fruit that looks so good to eat?

The answers were really not at all necessary to learn. The only thing that was necessary was obedience to God, who had made everything they saw and enjoyed. He is the Rightful Owner and as such, has every right to make the rules that He wants to make. Moreover, He also has every right to expect His rules to be followed.

Chapter 4

Look-Alikes and Copy Cats

Most people would not be able to tell the difference between the two jars above by simply looking at them. If both jars were completely clean with the exact same color lids, the difference would remain hidden. Only when each was held would the realization take place that one was made of glass and the other plastic. Looking at them simply says "I'm a jar!" Both jars act the same, look the same and can carry things inside them, from liquids to nails. However drop both empty jars onto the floor, and only one would shatter into pieces. The other may simply crack, but it would not react as the glass one would.

This simple illustration takes us into our next biblical parable: the Parable of the Wheat and the Tares, which is found only in the gospel of Matthew, chapter thirteen. It is in this parable that we get another glimpse of things from God's perspective.

A farmer sowed only good seeds of wheat during planting season. Unfortunately, an enemy wanted to ruin him financially, so under cover of darkness, he sowed seeds of darnel or tares, into the farmer's newly planted field.

Wait Until the Harvest
It was not until the wheat sprouted that the farmer realized there was a problem. As they grow, tares often wrap their stalks around and among the actual wheat, making it difficult to pull the tares out without damaging or removing wheat as well. It becomes much easier to separate the wheat from the tares, when the wheat is ready to be harvested.

When asked by his helpers if they should go through the field and pull out the *tares*, the farmer simply said, "*No, for while you are gathering up the tares, you may uproot the wheat with them. Allow both to grow together until the harvest; and in the time of the harvest I will say to the reapers, 'First gather up the tares and bind them in bundles to burn them up; but gather the wheat into my barn'*" (Matthew 13: 29-30).

These two parables (the Sower and the Wheat and Tares) teach us a number of things about individuals in the Church. They teach 1) that Jesus knew people would walk away from the faith, and 2) Jesus knew there would be individuals who were not actually true Christians who would become part of the Church.

It should be no surprise to us when this happens. Just as the tares are not *actually* wheat because they can grow right next to and among the wheat, neither are all who claim to be Christians actually Christians. They can and do attend church like Christians, speak like Christians and do other things that Christians do. These folks mingle with actual Christians in the Church, often causing problems in those individual churches and in the overall Church worldwide. This is not to say that everyone who "falls from grace" so to speak, is only a professing Christian. Obviously, a percentage of real Christians also fall by sinning in various ways.

Neither the world (or other Christians) of course sees any difference between the "professing" Christian and the actual or true Christian. Only God knows. This is exactly why a biblical church follows the discipline outlined in the New Testament for those who are found to be 'in sin.' There must be safeguards in place that a church can use to lovingly correct the fallen individual.

Those who refuse to place themselves under those measures of discipline are telling us something about their relationship (or lack of it) with Jesus. In fact, there *needs* to be accountability with people who oversee congregations. We are just asking for problems, without some type of accountability in place.

A person who rejects the idea of biblical accountability is really rejecting God's authority. Jesus Himself placed Himself under accountability, not only to God the Father, but to human beings! How do we get off by saying that we do not need to be accountable to others?

Of those who leave the church by rejecting Christianity, they have washed their hands of Christianity. In truth, these folks could easily be the "tares" with which the enemy has seeded the Church. Some however, may be simply backslidden, as seen in the Parable of the Prodigal Son.

Leaving in Droves
Jesus Himself experienced situations in which people left Him and never returned. In fact, it occurred on a fairly wide scale after He made a number of specific statement to the crowds He had been teaching one day. These statements shocked them into making a hasty retreat in disgust. It is recorded for us in the gospel of John, chapter six.

Beginning in verse twenty-two, we read of the situation in which crowds of people followed Him in boats across the sea to Capernaum. Jesus had fed this crowd of over 5,000 earlier. After they had finished eating and saw that it had been truly a miracle, they decided He was a prophet. ("Hey! This guy must be a prophet! He fed all of us! Let's make him king so we will always have food and never go hungry!") Jesus knew their thoughts, so He withdrew from the crowd and went to the foothills. The people wanted Him to be king because of what He had done *for* them; in providing food. They figured that if this guy could make food like that out of little or nothing, they would *never* go hungry again!

Heading Out for a Walk
Toward evening, when things had quieted down, Jesus walked across the water to Capernaum. His disciples had already gone on ahead of Him and we are all familiar with the story of Jesus telling Peter to walk out onto the water. Peter attempted it, and seemed at first to succeed, but then began to sink. This is due to the fact that he began to focus on his surroundings, which *drained* the little amount of faith he had. They all eventually made it to the other side of the sea and stayed there for the evening.

The next day, the crowds were back, trying to find Jesus. Not finding Him on one side of the sea, they got into boats and headed for the other side; the Capernaum side.

As Jesus met them after they reached the shore, He called attention to the fact that they were looking for Him solely because He had provided food for them. He then taught them the difference between food that we eat for physical sustenance and food that we "eat" for eternal life. Of course the people wanted that, so Jesus stated *"I am the bread of life; whoever comes to me shall not hunger, and whoever believes in me shall never thirst"* (John 6:35).

This particular statement did not go over well, because in verse forty-one we read that *"The Jews grumbled about Him..."* After telling them to stop grumbling, in verse fifty-one He states, *"I am the living bread that came down from heaven. If anyone eats of this bread, he will live forever. And the bread that I will give for the life of the world is my flesh."* Here is one of those statements in which Jesus either is who He says He is, or He is an idiot. It cannot be both ways. By calling Himself the bread of life, He is stating that He is God and that He can put them in a situation in which they will never hunger or thirst. This is the same as saying, "I am God and I can grant you eternal life." Jesus was saying that anyone who came to Him would *never* hunger or thirst. The use of the word *never* implies the opposite; the people would not be hungry for all of eternity. This is eternal life.

If Jesus was not God, then He had no business saying what He said. Certainly He would have known how the Jews would have understood His words. He said it anyway, which means 1) He was a moron who did not think the people would react the way they did, because that is not what He meant, or 2) He was a moron who knew how they would react, but was trying to get Himself killed by "blaspheming" [claiming to be God], or 3) He was God and had every right to say what He said.

"The Jews" (this term generally referred to the religious leaders), of course were focusing on His actual words and the *hyper-literal* meaning they took from those words, and responded in verse fifty-two with, *"How can this man give us his flesh to eat?"* People who are looking for mistakes and contradictions in Scripture will point to statements like these and make a foolish statement like "Christians are not really Christians if they are not eating Jesus' flesh." They are just as foolish as "the Jews" who asked the question first, a few thousand years ago.

In Catholicism, during the sacrament of the Lord's Supper, it is taught and believed that as soon as the priest begins saying the words of consecration, the elements actually become the blood and body of Jesus Christ. In effect, this is sacrificing Him over and over and over, as opposed to doing this sacrament only in His memory, as He indicated it should be done, during the Last Supper in the Upper Room. This belief dates back to the Council of Trent.

More Shocking Words from Jesus
But Christ is not done impacting their morning yet, by ruining their appetite. He follows the first statement with another one, just as powerful when He states, *"Truly, truly, I say to you, unless you eat the flesh of the Son of Man and drink his blood, you have no life in you. Whoever feeds on my flesh and drinks my blood has eternal life, and I will raise him up on the last day. For my flesh is true food, and my blood is true drink. Whoever feeds on my flesh and drinks my blood abides in me, and I in him"* (John 6:53-56).

Christ is unequivocally stating that we must eat his flesh and drink His blood. He does not just say it once either. He mentions it *four* times in that one paragraph. He obviously did not make a mistake and it is for this reason that *"many of his disciples turned back and no longer walked with him."* (John 6:66). It should be plain to see that since Christ was at this point in His ministry speaking in parables, and hyperbole, He meant something *other* than actually eating His flesh and drinking His blood. He was referring to His upcoming crucifixion, in which His body would be battered, bruised, and scarred. He would shed His blood for the remission of sins. Jesus is speaking of the need to *partake* of Him spiritually, by faith in His atoning act of death on the cross. He was not suggesting, commanding, or expecting people to become cannibals. He was emphasizing the *spiritual* need of the people and was simply saying that He was the answer to that spiritual need, if they would partake of Him, by understanding that His death is what provides eternal life.

Becoming a Christian

By faith we participate because we are saying *"Yes Lord, I believe that the only salvation available comes through and because of your death on the cross and resurrection from the grave.*

"I recognize and admit that there is nothing I can do to save myself. By faith, I receive your salvation, asking that you produce within me the new birth that you spoke about with Nicodemus. Change my heart. Change my desires. Grow my faith, so that I will become mature in You, serving You in boldness and with gladness.

"Help me to set myself and its desires aside. Help me to know and count the cost of being one of Your followers. I thank you that even though I may feel absolutely no different now, by faith, I know that your Holy Spirit lives within me and has created that new birth. Just as I know that I cannot save myself, I also know that I need to begin getting to know You because we are now in relationship. I need to get to know You through Your written Word and through prayer. I know that I need to relinquish the plans I may have for my own life and allow You to use me as You see fit. I know that I need to begin fellowshipping with other people who are also in relationship with You. I know that I need to trust You to complete in me, what You have begun today.

"Lord, I know that there will be difficult times ahead because I remain in a world controlled by Satan and his forces. By Your grace, I will remain faithful and continue to be conformed to Your image, so that Your character is created within me.

"I am so thankful that salvation is something that You alone do and not something that I need to rely on myself to accomplish. Help me grow.

"Help me praise you in spite of the circumstances in life. Help me to know You and help me to glorify You."

The point of relating this part of Scripture is to show that while He lived, walked and breathed on this earth, many who *began* to follow Him came to a point where they *ceased* following Him.

In the Last Days
In Paul's second letter to the believers in Thessalonica, he clarifies for them the situation surrounding the End Times. In that letter, he states *"Let no one deceive you in any way. For that day will not come, unless the rebellion comes first, and the man of lawlessness is revealed, the son of destruction, who opposes and exalts himself against every so-called god or object of worship, so that he takes his seat in the temple of God, proclaiming himself to be God"* (2 Thessalonians 2:3-4).

Paul indicates "that day" (referring to the Lord's Day, aka the Second Coming of the Lord), will not occur until "the rebellion" takes place. *The New Kings James Version* uses the term "falling away." *The New American Standard Bible* uses the word "apostasy." The overall meaning is the same. Paul is saying that in the End Times prior to Christ's Second Coming, there will be large numbers of people who fall or walk away from Christianity. Are they actual Christians, or simply ones who *profess* to know Jesus Christ? They obviously at some point identify with Jesus as one of His followers, but will also come to a point of choosing to no longer be identified with Him, as they leave Christianity.

Certainly, it is possible that this group will also include the type of individual that Peter speaks of in 2 Peter 3, when he refers to those who come "mocking" in the Last Days. Their big question will be

"Hey, whatever happened to that promise about Jesus returning? They've been saying that for centuries and still nothing! Where is He?!"

That is already being said in certain circles. In fact, in John Loftus' book, which we deal with in the next chapter, he alludes to it himself. It is fundamentally clear from Scripture that not all who hear the Word *receive* the Word, and even among those who *seem* to receive the Word, *they fall away* because they never truly began a relationship with Jesus.

To approach an ex-Christian telling them that they were "probably never a real Christian anyway" solves nothing. The certainty is that either they were Christians and fell away (and this author disagrees that this is a biblical possibility), or they were only *professing* Christians, by walking and talking as a Christian, joining in Christian-type events, without the actual needed change within. It would be more accurate if the ex-Christian simply said they *thought* they were at one point Christian, but have come to reject it.

Nonetheless, this falling away is something that was foreseen by the writers of Scripture, and by Christ Himself. They saw it and they spoke and wrote about it. The fact that there are people who say they are no longer Christians should not surprise anyone. While it might be disheartening, it is not an uncommon phenomenon and Paul indicates that a very large falling away will occur in the Last Days.

People stopped following Jesus, in spite of His miracles and in spite of the fact that He was there *with them* at the time. It should not be surprising then that people will choose to stop following Him today - Someone they have never physically seen, nor have they seen any of His miraculous works.

While it is never easy to watch someone deny the Truth, all that can be done in these situations is to pray for them, hoping that God will see fit in His sovereignty to open their eyes to their error.

Regardless, God will certainly be glorified in all things. As it states in Scripture, *"at the name of Jesus EVERY KNEE WILL BOW, of those who are in heaven and on earth and under the earth, and that every tongue will confess that Jesus Christ is Lord, to the glory of God the Father"* (Philippians 2:10-11; cf. Isaiah 45:23 and Romans 14:11).

Carl Sagan, Walt Whitman, Madalyn Murray O'Hair, Samuel "Mark Twain" Clemens, Thomas Edison, Albert Einstein, Alfred Hitchcock, Aldous Huxley, Charles Darwin, George Orwell, Joseph Campbell, George Carlin and a host of other atheists have already left this earth. They have also bowed their knee to the King of Kings and Lord of Lords: Jesus Christ, God the Son.

There are multitudes of others who have not yet bowed the knee in eternity because they still live here, but they *will* bow their knee, and that includes this author. The difference though, is that while Sagan, et al were *forced* to bow the knee, this author does so willingly and gladly.

Chapter 5

Freedom to Disbelieve...

John W. Loftus says he spent a good amount of time as a Christian preacher. This was until he "*could no longer use the term 'Christian' to describe his present beliefs or state of mind since he now doubts many Christian doctrines, beliefs and biblical inter-*

pretations he once formerly accepted as rock-solid truths."[3]

The title of John's book is *Why I Became an Atheist (a Former Preacher Rejects Christianity)*. It is fairly well written and certainly a thoughtful and insightful treatise on a subject that was undoubtedly difficult for him to come to put into words: going from Christianity to Atheism.

Why I Became an Atheist contains 428 pages in three parts, with twenty-four chapters. John titles the three sections, *Part I: The Basis for my Control Beliefs*; *Part II: The Biblical Evidence Examined*; and *Part III: What I Believe Today*.

Unfortunately, space does not permit us to write as much as we would like about the book, nor are we able to share as much *from* the book as we think reasonable. In spite of that though, we have endeavored to present as accurate a picture as possible with the amount of space we have set aside for it.

Catalysts
Loftus presents some interesting (as well as sad) events which took place in his life. Some of these he cites as catalysts which caused his ultimate withdrawal from Christianity. In fact, one has to admire his willingness to share so much of himself in print, at least some of which has likely come back to haunt him.

John narrows it down to three things that caused his complete and final rejection of Christianity: *"a major crisis, plus new information that caused [him] to see things differently, minus a sense of a loving, caring, Christian community."*[4]

---

[3] John W. Loftus, *Why I Became an Atheist,* (Amherst: Prometheus Books, 2008), 7
[4] Ibid, 24

He explains in some detail each of these particulars and how they served to bring him to a point of acknowledging what became severe doubts regarding Christianity. Eventually, John came to wonder why God had seemingly done nothing at all to *"avert these particular experiences of [his], especially if [God] could foreknow that [he] would eventually write this book and lead others astray?"*[5] To that of course, the question of "free will" needs to be considered.

Ultimately, John believes it was a *lack* of love within the Christian community that caused him to reject that for which he had previously been so passionate. He also obviously believes that God is to be blamed for not keeping certain things that occurred in his life from happening. Free will anyone?

No one can rationally argue *against* the point that there are many within Christendom who evidence no real love for one another, for the Lord, or for the lost of the world. This is a truth that Christians everywhere need to admit and address. If Christians are called to love as Christ loved, then that is the command. Yet, an answer does exist and it is clearly seen in Scripture. Did John not notice this answer, or if so, did he simply reject it?

The question then is why this love is not obvious in segments of the Christian community? It is safe to say that John is at least in some measure, confusing the *wheat* with the *tares*. Beyond that, while he was a Christian, John seems to have been completely oblivious to the fact that spiritual war rages around us. Where did he think persecution came from in general? How about the crowds that stoned Stephen, or Paul, or killed Christ, or beheaded this apostle or that one, or crucified hundreds of Christians and used them as torches to light gardens? What about the situation in the Corinthian church? Why

---

[5] John W. Loftus, *Why I Became an Atheist,* (Amherst: Prometheus Books, 2008), 31

would James feel the need to discuss the fact that true Christians should evidence the truth in their life by the way they live? Moreover, why would James feel it was important to connect this with the fact that antichrists and persecution exists, but that Christians should be patient in trials? Peter says as much, as does Paul, as does Christ.

Should we consider the Old Testament and the plans against Daniel with the lions, or his friends who were thrown into the fiery furnace? How about the troubles that Moses went through? What about Joshua? What about Hosea? It is difficult to know why the lack of love within the Christian community should act like such an exclamation point to John, or anyone else. It should have been an accepted fact that it exists, considering the truth that not all who are in the Christian community are in fact, Christians; a point which has already been thoroughly discussed at length.

What of the annals of history since Christ's time that highlight one Christian after another executed for his faith in Christ? What of those Christians down through the ages who gave up all they had to serve Christ, come what may?

Rather than attempting to belittle John's very real and hurtful situation, it needs to be placed within the context of *true* Christianity and the impact it has had on the world. Beyond this, the impact that true Christianity has had on its own followers cannot be understated.

Helping the Down and Out
John relates another one of the catalysts that prompted him to question and eventually reject Christianity. He speaks of being the founding president of a homeless shelter; a place in which he ministered to the down and out. This is certainly the type of ministering to people that Christ and others in the New Testament would agree is a necessary response to society on the part of those who call themselves Christian.

Christianity must be visible to the lost of the world and it can only be visible to them by the Christian's actions and words, which although they are outward signs, are necessary nonetheless.

While at the shelter, John also worked with a woman named Linda, who was the executive director there. He does not state whether or not he believed her to be a Christian. He does however talk about her willingness to serve and be what he needed her to be at the shelter. In fact, he indicates that *"she practically idolized [him]."*[6] That alone should have sent up a huge red flag to John.

Linda did things without complaining and was in many ways an individual who seemed to be thoroughly vested in serving John and the needs of the homeless.

Unfortunately (as can happen in situations like this), John and Linda became too close, and due to problems John was experiencing in his marriage, wound up succumbing to temptation and had an affair. This is tragic, and one cannot help but wonder why John was so busy helping others that his own relationship with his wife suffered as it did (if that was the case). Why did ministry seemingly come first, to the point that his own family seemed to take a back seat? In one of his letters to Timothy, Paul speaks against allowing this to happen.

John begins the next paragraph with an interesting statement: *"There's so much more I'd like to say about this, but few people would believe me."*[7] That is an interesting statement if for no other reason than the fact that he seems incredulous that no one believed Paul and Barnabas in a situation they found themselves in, as narrated in the Book of Acts. More on that later.

---

[6] John W. Loftus, *Why I Became an Atheist,* (Amherst: Prometheus Books, 2008), 25
[7] Ibid, 25

As John tells it, Linda had been involved in stripping for a living in the past and according to him, *"had it in for preachers."*[8] He relates that this situation could have been prompted by the fact that *"he was a moral crusader in town and stood against abortion and X-rated video rentals."*[9]

The Social Gospel

John was involved in spreading the *social gospel*. This is something many Christians mistake for spreading the *actual* gospel. The problem here is that things are backwards. Christians often fall into the trap of thinking that if they can simply change the *outward* appearance of the person or the world, then things will change *inwardly*.

John, like many others, unfortunately believe that if you change the circumstances that exist in a city, then it will follow that people's lives will change, because of a renewed *outward* moral climate. This is absolutely incorrect, and it is not the model that either Jesus or the apostles followed. It is certainly not what Jesus taught.

The idea is that if Christians get the porn shops closed, or get the strip clubs moved elsewhere, then an external situation is created which will allow or even prompt people to change. The problem with this is while it is fine to work to close down porn shops, and drug houses, and strip clubs, the reality is that these actions do not *change people*. Closing places down *does* change the neighborhood due usually to a reduction in crime (and that is a good enough reason to work eradicate these places), but it rarely changes the hearts of individuals. Christians though can sit back and congratulate themselves that they have accomplished something. But what have they accomplished?

---

[8] John W. Loftus, *Why I Became an Atheist,* (Amherst: Prometheus Books, 2008), 25
[9] Ibid, 25

John's narrative does not indicate exactly *how* he went about crusading against porn shops, so we are left to guess. Was he an angry crusader; a holier-than-thou individual, believing that the people who owned these business were worthless, lowlifes, deserving of hell and all the rest, or did he work quietly behind the scenes with the city government to eradicate the problem?

Since he was involved in a homeless shelter, it is obvious that he felt a sense of caring for the down and out. Ultimately we do not really know how John was viewed as a moral crusader, because he does not take the time to tell us how he worked against these businesses.

Dr. John MacArthur makes a noteworthy point here when he states *"We can sometimes invite persecution by being unduly abrasive and difficult, so that others do not persecute us as much for our faith as for the tacky way we express it. How can we tell the difference? Are people being offended by Christ or just by us? There is certainly no blessing in being obnoxious."*[10]

Christians should be on the front lines of course, but not in changing the way the city looks outwardly, as if that will usher in real and lasting change. Christians are called to help the poor, the hungry, those who are imprisoned, relieving as much suffering as we are able. It is our responsibility to do that and as part of that solution, the absolute *best* thing we can do for them is to introduce them to the only Person who can provide them with the thing they need most: *eternal life*.

The Christian's primary responsibility as seen in the life of Jesus and His apostles is to *serve* people by ministering to them on the spiritual level, *while* taking care to eliminate their physical needs, as we are able.

---

[10] John MacArthur, Grace for Today, Vol. 1, (Chicago: Moody Publishers, 2008), 86

The Christian today is too involved in spreading the social gospel, by getting outward things changed, instead of ministering to the needs of the less fortunate and those who are lost. As God changes the hearts of those involved in practices like stripping, or pornography, those things become part of their past, not their present. It is then that God may raise up some of *those* individuals to go back to those areas and minister to people who are like they once *were*; strippers, prostitutes, and the rest. Their testimony may be more effective in meeting their spiritual needs simply because they can relate to those who are still involved in it.

Christians need to be spreading *THE* gospel of Christ, not the social gospel of today's liberal Christian, who believes change starts on the outside. Some all too often believe that as we change the outward situations, we move closer toward a point in which Christ (as He rules in more and more hearts of men), will eventually rule in all the hearts of men. This in turn will usher in the "Messianic Millennium," which is understood to be a spiritual kingdom, not a physical one. The only way to get to this view is by allegorizing Scripture when there is no good reason to do so.

Yes, the Christian absolutely needs to be involved in meeting the needs of those who go without. The souls of the lost must always be uppermost in the mind of the Christian, not whether or not the local movie rental store rents porn. These endeavors are good, but they never take the place of evangelizing, which in turn saves souls. Again, while it is good in and of itself and there are numerous reasons for doing so, getting porn removed from stores does not save souls.

Potiphar's Wife and Joseph
John continues his narrative by comparing his situation with that of Joseph's when he was accused of attempted rape by Potiphar's wife (cf. Genesis 39). This got Joseph tossed into prison. When Potiphar's wife attempted to seduce Joseph he ran away from her as fast as he

could, leaving his cloak behind because of her death grip on it, not because he had removed it.

The temptress then used his cloak as evidence against him, building her tale on a lie. There was no trial. There was nothing even close to what people would normally consider to be justice. The circumstantial evidence used against him signed, sealed and delivered his fate.

It is difficult to see how John believes his situation is similar to that of Joseph's. Except for the fact that both men were falsely accused of rape, there are no other similarities. John created his own situation by entering into an extra-marital affair with Linda. Joseph did nothing to create the situation in which Potiphar's wife falsely accused him. Joseph went to jail and was essentially forgotten. John did not go to jail. Joseph did not get angry with people or God. In fact he realized that all that had happened to him was for good (Genesis 50:20-21). John however, felt betrayed by other Christians and God.

Even though John knows what he did was wrong (admitting that in his book), he has real difficulty with the fact that the lack of understanding by other Christians was so prevalent. John believes they should have been able to put themselves in his situation, which would have allowed them to understand the difficulty of it. He felt that he was all too quickly condemned by other preachers. He also believes that there were "mitigating factors here,"[11] which seem to be really nothing more than John attempting to excuse his behavior. This is what Adam did and it is what Eve did, and it is what we *all* do when having to face the mistakes we make.

David's Sin

Do we need to discuss David's life at this juncture? He sinned by committing adultery and then made it worse by attempting to cover

---

[11] John W. Loftus, *Why I Became an Atheist,* (Amherst: Prometheus Books, 2008), 25

that sin by creating another one: by having Bathsheba's husband Uriah killed in battle. This piled sin upon sin, and for a man of David's stature and relationship with the Lord, he absolutely should have known better. Did God forgive him? Yes, but the consequences of his actions remained. The reader is encouraged to read the full account in 2 Samuel 11 and following.

To begin with, David was in the wrong place. He should have been off leading his troops into battle, instead of being home in his palace. The text states very clearly here, "*In the spring of the year, the time when kings go out to battle, David sent Joab, and his servants with him, and all Israel. And they ravaged the Ammonites and besieged Rabbah. But David remained at Jerusalem.*" (II Samuel 11:1)

His decision to remain at home cost him many things. He was not being a good example for the soldiers who fought for and under him. Had he been with them, he would not have been bored at home, wandering around his roof, which overlooked the city.

Jerusalem was built on a hill with the palace of David at its highest point. It literally looked down over the entire city, making it easy to see the other rooftops. This is also why there are many references to going *up to* Jerusalem throughout the Bible, and it did not matter from which direction a person traveled. From any geographical point, one would travel *up to* Jerusalem.

Had David been off leading his troops, he would not have seen Bathsheba bathing and he would not have lusted. He would not have sent messengers to the woman and had her brought to him. He would not have slept with her, nor would he have impregnated her. He would not have tried to get Uriah to sleep with Bathsheba before going into another battle. Uriah showed more moral fiber than David as seen by his refusal to enjoy the company of his wife the night before a battle. He preferred instead to remain with his friends and fellow warriors in the bunkhouse the night before battle. (II Samuel 11:6-9)

David of course was hoping that Uriah would sleep with his Bathsheba, and make love with her. Her earlier pregnancy would be credited to Uriah and life would go on. Whew. David would have dodged the bullet on that one!

However, it did not work out like that, and upon learning that Uriah had not spent the evening with his wife, Bathsheba, David grew more concerned. He was concerned that his sin would be found out and he dreaded that prospect.

Becoming a Murderer
As a last resort, David committed the only thing he feels was left: murder. Murder?! Yes, murder. Here are some of the saddest words in the Old Testament: *"In the morning David wrote a letter to Joab and sent it by the hand of Uriah. In the letter he wrote, 'Set Uriah in the forefront of the hardest fighting, and then draw back from him, that he may be struck down, and die'."* (2 Samuel 11:14)

David really fell from the heights. Not only did he have Uriah killed by putting a "hit" on him, but David used Uriah to carry the note which contained his own death sentence! How utterly reprehensible, but David knew that Uriah's honor to the king would keep him from reading that note. Can you imagine the look on Joab's face as he took the note from Uriah and read it?

It is remarkable how often the Bible gets lambasted from every corner, yet the thing that is really interesting is how often the Bible shows people for what they truly are: wicked. The Bible does not attempt to hide that fact. Turn to just about any section of the Bible and the result is the same; seeing what people are truly made of. You would think that if the Bible was merely written by human beings, there would be *much* less emphasis on the failures and foibles of human beings. This is not the case though. Unlike Greek mythology, where people are often glorified, the biblical landscape is littered with people who fail and fail *mightily*, yet God forgives and restores.

Here is David in all his sinfulness and we see how far he had come: from man of honor, to man of murder. How terrible that this man who slew Goliath, was loved by God, and was shown *consistent* favor by God, could come to the point of having someone deliberately *killed*. For what? To cover his own sin. Friends, it cannot be stated how important it is to remain close to God, which is only accomplished through prayer and the study of His Word. *No one* is above falling. *No one* is beyond sinning. *Not one of us* is above doing things that serve only to cover our sin. It is all born of selfishness from the indwelling sin nature. Only by remaining as close in fellowship to God as we possibly can, are the chances of sinning like this reduced.

Nathan Speaks for God
Because David had fallen so far, and had stopped listening to that still small voice of conscience that God uses to express His moral will, it was necessary to send someone to speak to David. We read about this in II Samuel 12.

The prophet Nathan comes to David, the king of Israel, and relates a story about a rich man who stole from a poor man. The poor man had one sheep for his pasture and he loved that one sheep, like family. He cared for it and gave it some of the best food and made sure that all of its needs were cared for. The rich man was expecting company. Instead of taking one of his own flocks to use for dinner, this rich man, who had more than enough for himself with plenty of sheep, stole the poor man's sheep because he did not want to use one of his own as dinner.

David's response in II Samuel 14:5 is quite revealing: *"Then David's anger was greatly kindled against the man, and he said to Nathan, 'As the LORD lives, the man who has done this deserves to die, and he shall restore the lamb fourfold, because he did this thing, and because he had no pity.'"* Well, would you look at that. David's sense of righteous anger lit up like a Roman Candle against this obvious injustice. Of course, he failed to see that the story was about him.

In verse seven, we read these words spoken by Nathan: *"You are the man!"* David was, as we would say in today's vernacular, *owned* by Nathan. He was stunned and left speechless.

Read the remaining words of Nathan in verses seven to fifteen: *"Thus says the LORD, the God of Israel, 'I anointed you king over Israel, and I delivered you out of the hand of Saul. And I gave you your master's house and your master's wives into your arms and gave you the house of Israel and of Judah. And if this were too little, I would add to you as much more. Why have you despised the word of the LORD, to do what is evil in his sight? You have struck down Uriah the Hittite with the sword and have taken his wife to be your wife and have killed him with the sword of the Ammonites. Now therefore the sword shall never depart from your house, because you have despised me and have taken the wife of Uriah the Hittite to be your wife.' Thus says the LORD, 'Behold, I will raise up evil against you out of your own house. And I will take your wives before your eyes and give them to your neighbor, and he shall lie with your wives in the sight of this sun. For you did it secretly, but I will do this thing before all Israel and before the sun.' David said to Nathan, 'I have sinned against the LORD.' And Nathan said to David, 'The LORD also has put away your sin; you shall not die. Nevertheless, because by this deed you have utterly scorned the LORD, the child who is born to you shall die.' Then Nathan went to his house."*

Whew. What could David say in response to that indictment? What David had done in secret, God revealed publicly. Though God *would* forgive David these terrible sins, the *consequences* of the sins remained. Please note that God's punishment included a number of things which David would be powerless to stop:

- The sword would never depart (David's house would always be filled with strife and death);
- Evil would rise up against David from within his own family;
- God would take David's wives and give them to neighbors;

- The sin of David, done secretly would be done in the open by others;
- Finally, the baby that Bathsheba carried would die.

One must also notice God's indictment of David. He in no way lets him off the hook with but a slap on the wrist. God is speaking and says:

- I anointed you king over Israel;
- I delivered you out of the hand of Saul;
- I gave you your master's house and your master's wives;
- I gave you the house of Israel and of Judah;
- I would have added much more to that ("as if this were too little" – please do not miss the sarcasm here in God's voice);
- You have despised My words;
- You have done evil in My sight;
- You have struck down Uriah the Hittite with the sword;
- You have taken his wife to be your wife;
- You have killed him with the sword of the Ammonites;
- You have despised Me.

Please note that God repeats the accusations several times to underscore His absolute displeasure. Please also note that God is holding David *personally* responsible for Uriah's death, even though the Ammonites were the ones who actually plunged the sword into Uriah. God also takes these acts of sin personally. Why? Because God created man, and issued laws to guard the sanctity of man. Murder is man striking out at God, since man was made in God's image.

In that same chapter of II Samuel, David's newborn son died on the seventh day after his birth. No amount of pleading with God would change that fact. God turned a deaf ear to David and David finally realized that nothing would change regarding his son. Notice that the text states *"Then David arose from the earth and washed and anointed himself and changed his clothes. And he went into the house of the LORD and worshiped. He then went to his own house."* (II Samuel 13:20)

David was trying to get his life right before God. He was trying to do what he knew he should do. He harbored no anger against God or Nathan, knowing he had no right. He stopped pining for his son and acknowledged God's sovereignty.

When questioned by his confused servants about why he fasted and wept while the child was alive, but now that the child had died, he was eating (instead of mourning), David answered *"Can I bring him back again? I shall go to him, but he will not return to me."* (II Samuel 13:23b) Even though David understood that the child was gone from this life forever, he would see him again, after his own death in the next life.

In the very next chapter of II Samuel, we see God's Word further coming to fruition with David's son Absalom. Absalom winds up committing murder to defend his sister's honor. He did not stop there though, because he killed *"all the kings sons."* (II Samuel 13:30)

David mourned for Absalom (v. 30) because he knew that it was his own sin which caused Absalom to become what he had become. Absalom would be held responsible for his own murderous actions, but David would share the blame. Eventually, Absalom succeeded in turning the hearts of David's own men against him causing David to flee Jerusalem.

Consequences

As an aside, what John Loftus seems not to realize in his book is that he effectively canceled himself out of the ministry by engaging in a sin of that moral magnitude. He did not just hurt himself, but he hurt his wife, his co-worker Linda, and he sinned against the Lord. He did irreparable damage to his reputation. While the Lord obviously can forgive these sins, the consequences often remain, as we saw with David. Why does John believe that his circumstances were such that God should have been more helpful?

It seems that John would rather find a way to excuse himself even though he admits that what he did was wrong. In one paragraph following the narrative of the situation that led him into sin, he quotes ethicist Richard Taylor who states that while it is easy to condemn adulterers, it should be remembered that (according to him), the first real adultery in the relationship might have occurred not by the person who became physically involved with another individual, but by the one who may have withheld *love* that they had promised to extend during their marriage vows. This of course makes little sense. Taylor is effectively saying "I committed adultery, because *you* committed adultery. We are now even!" One sin does not cancel out another sin. It simply adds to it. The Christian is supposed to respond to sin with forgiveness and love. But because some might not respond in that manner, does not mean that God is held liable for it.

It needs to be asked, "Who cares what any 'ethicist' says?" The only ethicist that matters is the Supreme ethicist. That aside, it appears as if John is pointing to some of those mitigating circumstances he mentioned by implying that his wife withheld love (and possibly marital relations).

Because he was so busy with ministry (as one possibility), the absence of her love weakened him over time. He finally gave way to the temptation to become physically involved with someone other than his wife. In the end, it was really *her* fault though. Does this sound familiar? It was the same strategy that Eve used and then Adam. The only one who did not attempt to pass the buck was the serpent. He simply took his punishment without uttering a sound.

John further states that his illicit relationship went on for a bit; "*After only a few months, I finally decided I could no longer reconcile the af-*

fair with my faith or my family life. So I told Linda that it was over."[12] One has to wonder why it took him a few months to come to the awareness that what he was involved in was against God's commands. During that time, he apparently found some way to rationalize it so the affair could continue.

As one can imagine, breaking things off with Linda caused the beginning of public problems for John. Linda went to the city prosecutor as well as John's former associate minister and accused John of raping her. No charges resulted from it, although people wondered about the truth of the accusations. He says he received a death threat over the phone, while others whom he knew and respected simply did not know what to believe. John was tremendously hurt by this entire situation and from the reactions of others who also considered themselves to be Christians.

It is important to note though that what John experienced was caused by himself. It seems that he agrees with this, but the excuses he throws into the mix leave the impression that though he sinned, it should have been forgiven and forgotten with life going on. Christians (real or not) are *not* exempt from consequences of their actions in this life.

Giving Up on Faith

What John went through obviously caused him pain, but there are many Christians who go through situations far worse. Yet, not only do they *not* reject their faith, they often grow *stronger* in their faith because of those situations. This difference needs to be addressed as well.

The reader should take note that this discussion of John's situation was highlighted for two reasons:

---

[12] John W. Loftus, *Why I Became an Atheist,* (Amherst: Prometheus Books, 2008), 27

1. John had already publicly related the events in his book, making it common, public knowledge, and
2. To discuss what appears to be faulty logic related to these events, from a biblical standpoint.

It cannot be stated strongly enough that this author has not included and discussed these particular events in John's life in order to condemn, or judge him. It is also not the intent to make John feel as if this author stands above him morally. The reality is that *all* have sinned and *all* have fallen short of God's glory as Paul proclaims in Romans. This author is just as needy of Christ's forgiveness and His salvation because of his own sin nature and individual sins, as is John and every other person in life.

It is often easier to see the truth of the situation when one is not directly involved in it, as with Nathan and David. It is understood that for this author, others would (and do) see things that need to be addressed easier than the author sees them with respect to his own life. This is one of the greatest reasons why fellowshipping with other (true) believers is important, as is being open to God's chastising hand, and being willing to place one's self under the authority of a local church body.

Accountability must exist for every Christian, or that Christian will fail miserably in maintaining fellowship with Christ and purging his life of the sin that so easily traps us. In his letters to the Corinthian believers, Paul outlines how to "discipline" a wayward believer and ultimately how to bring that same believer back into fellowship through forgiveness and restoration. Paul outlines these instructions because of specific situations occurring at Corinth, and also because there is not one person who is above succumbing to temptation and falling. The church needs to know how to lovingly discipline, and Christians need to be aware that they must be held accountable.

John presents his situation with a type of reasoning in which he obviously feels that the punishment was worse than the "crime." While it may look and feel that way to John, the reality is that this is simply the way people act. And since we know that the church is filled with professing Christians (posers) who are not truly Christians (tares), they especially have no power to react as Christ would react in these situations.

The fact that John uses the lack of Christian love as one of the reasons he left Christianity is simply not a meritorious argument, nor is it one based on logical reasoning. Christ never says Christians are instantly made perfect. Neither does He say that Christians will always err on the side of caution and good, as opposed to evil. Christians are people who have been forgiven and who have been given a new start in life, made possible through the new birth. The process of *perfecting* does not conclude in this life.

The fact that Christians may not be as loving as people think they should be provides no excuse at all, because not one of Jesus' followers will ever reach perfection *in this life*. Christians are all capable of making bad decisions, doing terrible things and not loving as they should. *Every* Christian proves that. John proved that, yet even though *he* sinned and fell short of God's glory, he believes he can excuse his rejection of Christianity by blaming it on the fact that many *other Christians* acted just as human as he did. How is that even close to being rational?

Christ is the example. He is the model; the expression of love. Christ was and is the epitome of love at every turn. Looking at just the last few days of His life, we see a Man falsely accused of blasphemy, deserted and rejected by those who said they loved Him, betrayed by another, deprived of sleep, food, and water, slapped around, spit upon, literally beaten to a pulp, his back shredded open, and finally nailed to a cross to die. One of the things He said from the cross was this:

"Father, forgive them because they do not know what they are doing." THIS is love. THAT is the example. It is something we should strive to reach, but will never do so perfectly in this life.

The Christian's Superiority Complex
John moves on to deal with what he feels is a superior attitude held by Christians regarding their beliefs and the moral foundation upon which Christianity is built. He feels that many Christians, because of what they believe, place themselves above all other religious systems. John rightly points out that many of the great minds of science and thought over the centuries have been atheists. While this is true, there have also been (and currently are) many Christians in these areas too, and John notes that. This proves Scripture, because God sends rain to the just and the unjust (cf. Matthew 5:45). This simply points out the truth that God will bless humanity with "good gifts," whether they are Christian or not. In that regard, certainly God is no respecter of persons.

John's point seems to be that Christians should *not* have a superior attitude because there are many outside Christianity who are moral and brilliant. Christianity does not have a corner on either of these areas. That is another true statement.

It has been this author's experience that there are people within Christendom (just as in the world at large), who are manipulative, licentious, and generally do things that Christians should *not* do. Paul wrote to some people like this in the church at Corinth. This argument, though, does *not* negate the veracity of Christianity. It simply negates the integrity of that particular individual.

Interestingly enough, the arguments that John espouses really do not have the effect that he may have hoped, at least on this author. It is true that God has blessed both groups (Christian and non) with genius and high moral fiber. There are the opposites in those groups within Christianity and within the non-Christian community as well;

those possessing less than brilliant intelligence, and those with little to no moral fiber. This is not an essential argument that speaks for or against authenticity, or lack of it, with respect to Christianity.

John's arguments are based on man's view of morality, being merely philosophical in nature. This makes sense to him since he is an ex-Christian and prides himself in the area of apologetics and philosophy. The problem of course is that once God is taken out of the picture, there is really no cognitive difference between the moral codes or ethics from one group to the next, since all stem from man's thinking. One is not necessarily better than another, secularly speaking.

The Christian and the Mission
At the same time, it is important to note that not a few Christians have put their time, money and effort where their mouths are, by doing things *for* those in the world who are disenfranchised.

People like General William Booth who began the Salvation Army, John Wesley, who believed the only real holiness was social holiness. Millard Fuller (Habitat for Humanity), John Wanamaker (Christian Commission), George Mueller (Bristol England Orphanages), D. L. Moody (Worked Among America's Poor), Healing Hands Int'l, Martin Luther (Reformer: Stood Against Catholicism), John Calvin (Reformer: Stood Against Catholicism), William Tyndale (Executed: Stood Against Catholicism), Hudson Taylor (Missionary to China), Good Samaritan Health Center, Global Harvest Outreach, William Carey (Father of Modern Missionaries), Isaac Newton (Scientist), Mother Theresa (Nun Dedicated to Helping Poor), Ron Sider (Evangelicals for Social Action), United People in Christ, Inc., Operation Blessing International, Kingscare, Grace Ministries Overseas Aid, Helping Up Mission (Provides Hope to the Poor and Homeless), Joni Eareckson Tada (JAF Ministries: Disabilities Ministry), Great Commission Air, Marin Luther King, Jr. (Civil Rights Minister), African American Self-Help Foundation, Beyond Borders, Bread for the World, Beyond Tears Worldwide, Christian Mission Aid, Christian

Relief Services, Common Grace, Eastern European Aid Mission, Family Care Foundation, Global Samaritans, Healing Hands International, Hope for the Suffering, Heart for Africa, HOPE Worldwide, Interfaith Refugee Ministry (IRM), Joy of a Child, Mildmay HIV & AIDS Care, Mission Impossible, Mission without Borders, My Brother's Keeper, Pamoja, Samaritan's Purse, World Hope International, The Stephen Ministry (Caregiving Ministry), World Relief (International Poverty and Hunger Relief), World Relief Canada, and *thousands* of other groups were started by Christians who lived their lives the way Christ lived His: by considering the needs of others *first*.

The above organizations as well as others not listed, have taken the words of Jesus Christ seriously and literally when He said that to preach to the poor and disenfranchised without helping to meet their physical needs is worthless. Without organizations like those listed, this world would be a poverty-stricken mass of suffering humantiy, *much more* than it is currently. Again though, while these are good in and of themselves, people also need to be told about the salvation made possible through Jesus Christ.

The Atheist and Good Works
But what of the atheist or evolutionist? There are probably *some* helping organizations founded by people from these two groups. But it must be noted that the atheists have *no real motivation* to help anyone except themselves. In general, they *believe* nothing exists beyond this life. Their thinking is based on the evolutionary model which at its core, is the process of out-surviving another species by being more fit. What possible motivation is there for an atheist to help anyone (and *that* is the Achilles' Heel of atheism)? Due to their thinking, they have essentially become their own highest authority. There is no one higher than the atheists because nothing exists outside of the material world, according to them.

Just ask Madalyn Murray O'Hair, or Michael Newdow, or any other atheist that can be found. What did O'Hair accomplish with her life that relieved the suffering of humanity, besides forming American Atheists, getting school prayer abolished and whiting out the word "God" on the dollar bill? Since 1960, O'Hair was involved in one lawsuit after another (at taxpayer's expense).

In 1963, she made a hasty retreat from Maryland after assaulting five police officers. Later she filed suit against NASA because astronauts on Apollo 8 had the temerity to read from Genesis. In 1995, O'Hair was murdered. So ends her life here. But the point is, what good came from O'Hair's life? Prayer was abolished in school. Whoopee.

There are undoubtedly some atheists who have accomplished some good for humanity, but rarely do they ever help alleviate real suffering in this world. They will often be the first to tell you that *churches* should relieve suffering. When you do hear of them being involved in some project as philanthropists, it is usually splashed over the newspapers to be seen by everyone. That is their reward. True Christians though, have been involved behind the scenes for centuries, steadily working to eradicate this problem or that.

Recently, an international magazine included an article about why the average person should be involved in social causes. Apparently, science has now found that being involved in *good* activism can help a person *physiologically*. That is just swell. One woman took the time to found an organization that helps people who are left feeling as though they are at the mercy of the airlines. The article intones *"Giving a donation or volunteering in a food bank tweaks the same pleasure source that lights up when we eat or have sex."*[13]

---

[13] Meredith Maran, The Activism Cure, *MORE Magazine*, March 2009, 138

The article continues with more brilliant insight from the scientific community: "*Scans show that the brain structures that are activated when you get a reward are the same ones that are activated when you give. In fact, they're activated more.*"[14] And there you have it; the *real* reason why people should be involved in activism. Not because it helps others, but to help the *giver feel better*. What can one expect from a secular, materialistic society where individuals are taught over and over again to meet their own needs *first*?

The types of activism the average person is involved in today rarely move them out of their comfort level. Certainly some organizations created by folks to help society are good in and of themselves. However, whether it is MADD (Mothers Against Drunk Driving), or creating the Coalition for an Airline Passenger's Bill of Rights, these things come into being normally because the founder was personally affected by something that left them "scarred," or "traumatized," not because they saw a need and decided to meet it simply because the need was there and they could do something about it.

In the case of the Airline Passenger's Bill of Rights, the founder Kate Hanni came up with the idea after being stuck on a plane that sat on the tarmac for nine hours. There were no working toilets, no food and no water. Realistically, no one would deny that it was a terrible situation. However, that type of "suffering" in no way compares to those who are orphaned, homeless, starving to death, dying of AIDS, or disenfranchised on any level throughout the world. Organizations like those highlighted in the magazine article are born out of a desire to relieve the suffering a person feels for *himself*. Would these same folks be willing to lay down their lives for their organization? Of course not.

---

[14] Meredith Maran, The Activism Cure, *MORE Magazine,* March 2009, 138

Christians over the centuries have literally laid down their lives, or at the very least, given up their own comforts so that others might gain some semblance of comfort. They have done so simply because there is suffering in this world, and because of man's *inherent worth* which stems from a God-centered world view, not a man-centered one. True Christians (as opposed to the *pretenders*, the *wannabes* and the *posers*), have been on the front lines in their attempts to diminish suffering wherever it has been found since the time of Christ.

Deluded?
In spite of all that Christianity has accomplished in this world, John and other atheists prefer to sit back, look down their haughty noses and pronounce that Christians are deluded. Case closed. Who has the *real* superiority complex: the Christian or the atheist?

Frankly, this author would rather be "deluded" in thinking that because man was made in God's image, that he is of *infinite worth*. It is because of that worth that man is worth saving, whether from starvation or nakedness, or peril, or sword. Certainly he is worth saving from *hell*.

To the atheist/evolutionist, man is viewed as no such creature. Ultimately, man is as valuable as mud. Abortion? No problem. Murder? Sad, but it happens as part of that survival of the fittest instinct. Selfishness? Of course. What else can be expected of creatures who have evolved over "millions" of years and done so only by being able to *best* the other competitors? This type of thinking (or *rationale* if you prefer) is at best pitiful, and at worst self-aggrandizing. It promotes nothing but a self-centered laissez-faire attitude as far as the rest of the world is concerned.

A Giant Umbrella
John further makes the mistake of grouping all of Christendom under the same roof or umbrella. This difficulty seems to arise, and is exacerbated by, John's own lack of understanding when it comes to the

Bible and history. He frequently pulls verses out of context, comparing and contrasting, and ending up with results that simply do not hold up under careful exegesis. John does not seem to be purposefully unfair in his assessment of Christianity, or of the Bible and or of God. He seems to be doing his level best to show that *perceived* discrepancies in the Bible and in the lives of Christians have created a strong sense of hypocrisy that has not gone unnoticed by people outside (or even inside) the church. The difficulty though, is that the result is the same: his condemnation is based on faulty judgment.

However, while the argument remains that Christians seem to hold to a superior moral foundation and ethic, it is just as important to note that many atheists have what they tend to project as a superior brilliance over not only Christians, but those who are religious (read: superstitious). In fact, atheists and evolutionists believe they have extricated themselves from the antiquated myths, fables and superstitions which they believe are represented within Christianity, while the Christian still struggles to hold onto them, against all fact and reason.

The underlying difficulty is that nothing in John's book is based on any type of *spiritual transaction* that may have taken place in the Christian. This comes to the fore again and again throughout his book. Everything is seen from man's point of view, with no *spiritual context* or *significance*. It cannot be otherwise for John though, since he is an atheist, having disavowed God.

John's Testimony
While it might be in there, the author of this book did not find a specific spelled out description of just exactly how John became a Christian. The closest we get to it is when he states on page twenty of his book that he "accepted Jesus" and then tells us what he did after that. What exactly does "accepted Jesus" mean *to John*? What is John's definition here? He says His life changed and he began attending youth groups and became involved with other Christian friends. He even-

tually became a "Jesus Freak" which was often seen then as a way of rebelling against the establishment. His path led him to become baptized and ordained, and then onto a Christian college.

It was then that he began to read books by Josh McDowell, Hal Lindsey, and Francis Shaeffer. These convinced him even more that Christianity was factual. (It is too bad that he believes Hal Lindsey helped convince him about the veracity of Christianity and the Bible, because Lindsey has unfortunately made far too many errors over the years in area of prophecy.) John maintains he had no doubts about Christianity at this point. Later, upon looking back, he found these works riddled with discrepancies, and not at all convincing regarding the reality of Christianity. *"Five years later... I would find myself in the throes of doubt."*[15] But much of this (especially Francis Shaeffer's work) stems from areas related to the philosophical. Philosophy does not deal in facts per se. It deals in conversation, conjecture, thought and reason, which is only as good as the person involved in it. Since man is *finite*, then it *should* stand to reason that he will *never* be able to figure out the existence of God, or other things too ethereal to wrap his brain around.

Getting back to the moral code that John references, it is true that Christians have a moral code they follow as do the atheists, based on their belief systems. Again, take God out of the picture (because Loftus no longer believes that God in any form exists), and Christianity is like any other system of morals; *nothing more than manmade principles.*

---

[15] John W. Loftus, *Why I Became an Atheist,* (Amherst: Prometheus Books, 2008), 23

John also spends a good amount of time dealing with philosophy of religion, which *"attempts to analyze and critically evaluate religious beliefs."*[16]

Because of his current beliefs, he states that without any hard evidence to support Christianity, it should not be believed. The *"only evidence allowed is either evidence that is provided by direct experience or an argument based upon inferences from experience."*[17] If we go by that definition, one wonders why Evolution is as universally accepted as it is, since it has not been proven beyond doubt, nor has it been able to explain how life originated on this planet. Moreover, what about many of the laws within nature, that prior to being "discovered" worked fine, yet people did not know they existed? There was no proof in essence, yet they worked. Now we know how gravity works, but gravity was always there.

At the same time, why would the evidence of "direct experience" be allowed? That makes no sense because experiences can be faked, they can be self-created and they can be misunderstood.

No one was there to actually see or experience the beginning of life here, and so far as is known, no one has ever *witnessed* one of the adaptations as it supposedly happened within the Evolutionary model from one species to another. Within the same species is one thing, but where is the evidence that suggests adaptations occurred from one species to another?

Scientists are busy providing their 'statements of fact' based merely on *inferences*; however those inferences are not based on first person knowledge, but upon circumstantial evidence. They are based on fossil remains and other things; all circumstantial evidence at best.

---

[16] Ibid, 46
[17] John W. Loftus, *Why I Became an Atheist,* (Amherst: Prometheus Books, 2008), 47

We generally see no transitional fossil forms between different species of plants or animals. Only a few fossils that are *stated* to be (not proven to be) transitional have been reported, but the vast majority that one would think *would* exist are non-existent (scientists would say they simply have not been found yet, but the results that have not been proven are accepted as if they were proven).

Unfortunately, Darwin's entire premise for evolution – that evolution can change one type of organism into another – is simply not supported by the evidence. *"We observe microevolution both in nature and purposeful domestication within species. We do not observe macroevolution."*[18] Scientists, biologists and evolutionists disagree vehemently, yet it remains that they offer nothing as proof that the above statement is incorrect.

Early in his book, John explains how he came to believe that scientists are correct regarding the age of the earth and universe. This really presupposes that *if* God exists and *if* God created, He would not have created anything with the *appearance of age*. It is difficult to believe that God would have created things *without* the appearance of age. The Bible does not say that God created the heavens and the earth *six days ago*. It says He created everything *within six days*.

Would not God have created with the appearance of time? Surely if God created the heavens and the earth, the earth though only a few hours old, would have looked like it had existed for eons, would it not?

Likewise with the animals and Adam. Were they created as one-celled animals and allowed to develop into some higher life form, eventually gestate, hatch/be born, grow and establish themselves into adulthood? Would not God have created *full grown* animals and

---

[18] Rose Publishing, *Creation & Evolution* (Torrance: Rose Publishing 2005), 6

a full grown Adam and Eve? Would He have created the chicken or the egg first? Obviously, the chicken. Why would God create something only to have to wait until it *got to the point* of actually *being* millions or billions of years in age?

The age of the earth proves nothing really, except that it is old. But that appearance can be artificial. A God who actually created the universe would likely have created it with the appearance of age.

The Anti-Supernatural Bias

John eventually states what he feels best delineates his set of *control beliefs*: *"1) There is a strong probability that every event has a natural cause, and 2) the scientific method is the best (and probably the only) reliable guide we have for gaining the truth, even though I realize there is a fair amount of debate on just what that is..."*[19]

He feels that the scientific method is the best method for determining truth, even though by his own admission, the actual definition of truth remains elusive. Unfortunately, science has its limits and because of that it cannot prove or disprove certain things. It is unable to determine if the spiritual realm exists all. Because it cannot *detect* it, does not mean it does not exist.

Likewise, because science has not proven or become aware of God's existence, it does *not* follow that the default position is that God does not exist. From a Christian's perspective, it is obvious that there is an entire body of truth completely outside the ability of science to discern. If one sticks only with science in that case, that truth will never be discovered or understood. Then again if the spiritual realm could be proven, there would be no need for faith.

---

[19] John W. Loftus, *Why I Became an Atheist,* (Amherst: Prometheus Books, 2008, 59

In the final analysis, John has gone from taking Christianity on faith, to taking science on faith; or those things which fall into either of his two control beliefs. While he believes he has exchanged faith for reason, he has not. It *would be true* if the spiritual realm had been proven *not* to exist, but this has not occurred. Science does not *believe* the spiritual realm exists because it cannot be determined or measured empirically. Since it cannot be determined or measured empirically, science is unable to provide a verdict one way or another. *Believing* is the best they can do. While they might offer any number of reasons why they *believe* it does not exist, they cannot prove that it does not exist. They are left with believing that it does not exist. All of their arguments lead them to this conclusion, but those are merely philosophical arguments, not ones empirically-based; nothing more and nothing less.

When John or any other atheist makes the statement "God does not exist," what they are in fact actually saying or meaning is they do not *believe* God exists. They consider philosophical arguments for and against, along with any circumstantial evidence they find, from which they gain meaning and finally, they make a determination. Have they proven it as one would prove the existence of gravity? Of course not. We will delve more deeply into this area later in this book.

John considers his set of control beliefs to *"be the Achilles' heel of Christianity."*[20] That sounds as though he has created a slam dunk, putting the Christian in an untenable position from which he is unable to extricate himself, but he has not. Look where John starts. His very propositions look as if they offer him no security in his thinking. The reason for this is due to his use of the phrases *"a strong probability,"* or *"probably the only one,"* or *"there is a fair amount of debate."* There is nothing in his control beliefs even remotely suggesting sure-

---

[20] John W. Loftus, *Why I Became an Atheist,* (Amherst: Prometheus Books, 2008), 62

ty or provability. John himself does not *know*, nor can he *prove* that every event has a natural cause and he admits as much. It is impossible to do so and John knows it. Because he cannot do this, his control belief number one is no more a threat to Christianity than this author saying he can walk on water only to learn that he cannot. Just because John (or anyone else) has come up with artificially established control beliefs which rely on probability or the imperfection of the scientific method (due to its limitations), this in and of itself does not counteract Christianity, or the existence of God. It simply negates Christianity and God as viable *for the atheist*.

We Do Not Know
The scientist is allowed to say "we do not know…yet" and this is not seen as disingenuous, nor is it seen as thwarting belief in something that is said to be fact (though completely unproven, as in evolution). A scientist will give this type of response to a query regarding the lack of proof of something (the origin of life, as an example).

The statement "we do not know…yet" is used as a buffer to negate further questioning and to give the impression that a solution is consistently and currently being sought. It is given and inferred to be sufficient enough. The inference is that a truly wise person will understand and need nothing further because of what is known *so far*. If and when the time comes that absolute proof is found, or an answer provided, *then* a specific answer will be relayed. Until such a time, simply *believe* that the event which took place is a natural occurrence and its source (or the origin of life), though currently unseen and therefore unknown, will one day be seen and known. This is exactly what evolution expects us to believe and most are gullible enough to believe it, accepting it on *faith* (which is *knowing* what cannot be seen).

There are many things within nature and science that have absolutely no rational explanation, yet this is perfectly fine with the scientist, the skeptic and the atheist. They are allowed to have their *seasons of faith* when they can point to nothing specific as a reason why something took place, or simply shrug their shoulders and say *"We don't know, but we will one day as technology advances."*

The Christian though, far from being allowed to have or use faith, is seen as some superstitious loon who, going against reason and proof itself, holds on valiantly to a belief based on faith, in spite of all the supposed evidence to the contrary. The trouble is that many of the beliefs that the Christian holds to by faith have *not* been proven to be *incorrect*. They are simply either doubted, or disbelieved altogether.

Testing for Faith
John speaks of the fact that many faiths and religions exist. The question then becomes which one is the real one (if only one is real)? He believes that in large part, different faiths are chosen based on the culture or sociological background of the individual. It certainly stands to reason then that an individual born into a family which had been faithfully practicing Buddhism for centuries, would continue in that particular faith and practice. That makes sense. This in and of itself though, does not solve the problem of people who spend years growing up faithfully adhering to their families' religion (which became their own religion) only to one day break away and become Christian, or something else entirely. This actually works against John's theory.

This particular argument is really not a genuine argument. Of all the religions that exist, or ever have existed, Christianity is the only one in which its Founder is said to have come in order to die so that others might inherit eternal life. This author can think of no other religion that proclaims this. (Oh, and the idea that Christianity came from Mithras is so absurd that it is pointless to even discuss here, as other works have dealt with that quite sufficiently.)

Moral High Ground
The argument is also not genuine (and it does not even matter if Ri-

chard Dawkins claims that it is), because what the Christian is *not* talking about is a person having *any faith*. The Christians is talking about a person having *the true faith*. This is where it sounds like the Christian has a superiority complex. Yet when all is considered, Christianity has a high moral ground solely because of Jesus Christ, not because of the Christian, or anything the Christian has done. That moral ground is not necessarily seen in what people do (or do not do) in their daily lives. The moral ground is seen in the example of Jesus Himself who laid down His life for the remission of sins. Is that something that can be seen? Is that something that can be proven? The answer would be 'no' to both questions. Even in proving beyond a doubt that Jesus actually died on a cross does not prove that His death was for the remission of sins. Some do not even believe that Jesus actually lived at all. This is where faith plays a major role, and you cannot have true Christianity without faith.

If Christianity in fact begins with an actual spiritual transaction, it stands to reason that this spiritual transaction is the beginning from which the character of Christ is recreated within each Christian. In essence, the Christian is giving up his own morals, allowing them to be replaced with Christ's morality. This is a process that will continue for the remainder of our earthly lives and that progress depends upon how much the Christian is *willing to submit to God*. It also stands to reason that if the world hated Christ because of His moral fiber, the world will hate His followers if that same moral fiber is being recreated within each true Christian.

How a person comes to adopt their faith has nothing to do with anything. Atheists and skeptics alike are completely missing the point. Someone actually had to do a study on this? This is news? It is *obvious* that people gravitate toward one particular faith as opposed to another largely because of family, and in the absence of family, it would be because of friends. Christians have no difficulty with this proposition, nor should they have.

John seems to be leaving out something extremely important as well and it is because as he says, he is now an outsider to Christianity and from the outside it makes absolutely no sense to him (which argues against the fact that he ever was a true Christian). John is ignoring the fact (from a Christian perspective) that salvation is *not a matter of doing things*, or holding to one moral ground or another. It is a transformation of the human spirit, beginning with the new birth (spiritual transaction).

Looks Can Be Deceiving
Why do so many people within Christendom act not like Christ, but like the devil? Clearly, at least one answer has to do with the truth seen in the Parable of the Sower. Who would argue (except the atheist or skeptic), that *everyone* who attends church and even believes themselves to be Christian *is truly* Christian? Jesus points out (as well as Paul and others), that wolves in sheep's clothing will (not might, but *will*), enter the Church. Their goal is to destroy it from within. Why is this something that atheists readily seem to ignore, or are unable to comprehend? Is it because if they ignore the answer, they do not have to recognize the potential merit of the answer itself? If it can be shown that not everyone in the church is actually a Christian, then the argument that the Christian community is not all that loving begins to lose its force and validity.

The church is filled with fakes, wolves, charlatans and the like. It is clear that *if* God exists and *if* Jesus Christ came, lived, died and was resurrected, then Satan and his cohorts exist as well. If this is true then would not Satan spend all of his time trying to destroy the very thing that God was intent on creating? Would Satan not try every way possible of robbing people of salvation even before they receive it, and should they hear about it would he not do everything he could to make them doubt it and ultimately reject it?

Anyone who honestly thinks that everyone who attends church or says they are Christian are, in fact Christian, is someone who is deceiving themselves. It is patently *not* true. The church is filled with *tares*.

When the Church tries to use biblical methods to discipline wayward members often because of all the tares in the Church, the world claims the church has no love! Yet, if the Church does nothing with those who are living carnal lives then the world yells, "What a bunch of hypocrites!"

Another difficulty with John's reasoning is that when he refers to the atrocities that took place during the Middle Ages as one example, he refers to those people who perpetrated them as *Christians*. Yet in point of fact, what we saw during that period was the result of the Papacy and the Catholic Church and their corrupt *political* power. What does *that* have to do with the way Jesus Christ lived His life here on earth? There is no connection.

It is interesting to note that prior to the development of the Catholic Church (during the late third, early fourth century), the Church had one set of beliefs. With the onset of Roman Catholicism, Christianity took on a new set of beliefs, form and flavor altogether. One of those beliefs was that Roman Catholicism now assumed itself to be the new "Israel," and all the previous promises made to Israel were now transferred to the Church. Roman Catholicism now had the power to decide literally who would live and who would die (because the Church was God's "chosen nation" and arm of judgment, authorized to be judge, jury and hangman!), just as Israel had the power by God to eradicate any and all groups in Canaan centuries before. Anyone who failed to become Roman Catholic, or had the temerity to question the authority of Roman Catholicism, or stand in its way during that time could easily lose their lives and many did, through burnings at the stake, and other gruesome forms of execution.

This is exactly *why* despots like Adolph Hitler can refer to themselves as "Christian" and believe it is okay to kill Jews (or whomever). By God's authority, they can remove God's perceived "enemies."

This was *not* Christianity that perpetrated those terrible things. It was the Roman Catholic church's heretical policies. It is interesting to note that many Roman emperors took pleasure in torturing and killing Christians because it was fun or entertaining, or in the case of Nero, because he needed scapegoats to cover his insanity. Many emperors who were supposedly Christian after Christianity became the state religion were the furthest thing *removed from* Christianity.

When Constantine married the church to the state, Roman Catholicism got the boost of its life, lifting itself high above all other powers, ruling over everyone and using the power of the state and crown to do it. Everything was squelched and the Bible taken away.

This is *not* the Christianity that Jesus Christ introduced into the world. Every age since the Church's inception (which began in Acts 2) has had its own unique error that has never been completely overcome or eradicated. By far, the Roman Catholic Church introduced some of the greatest heresies into Christendom which still exist today. They *continue* to believe and espouse that salvation is by grace, through faith, plus works.

The Reformers who fought against the abuses of the clergy of Rome, as well as the heretical beliefs they espoused (indulgences, salvation by faith plus works, etc.), were either harassed unmercifully, or tortured, or executed. The list is a long one of those Christians who fought against the dogma of Roman Catholicism, losing their lives in the process. William Tyndale was burned at the stake by Roman Catholic officials for daring to go against the Pope by translating the Bible into the common language. There are too many others to list here. *This was not Christianity.*

John's book seems to become less profound and more pedantic as we move through it. At one point, he states *"The Christian theist must now try to rationally explain it"*[21] (referring to Jesus' death on the cross making salvation possible, by saving people from their sins). Why, because John says so? To do this says John, the Bible must essentially be tossed out and an attempt should be made to show that Jesus was fully God and fully Man, from a rational standpoint.

That is nonsense. It is completely idiotic. What John is actually stating is that we should take what is believed to be an all-knowing, all-powerful, eternal God and make Him understandable to humanity without using His Word to do it. How does one possibly fit the eternal into the finite? That is a rational absurdity, yet this is what John wants to leave the Christian with.

The Bible merely scratches the surface, regarding God, His character and His attributes. How is it possible to explain a mystery about why God chose to save, or how He chose to save, or how it works that God became man, yet still existed as fully God and fully Man? Even if it could be completely explained, finite minds would never be able to fully *grasp* it.

This is what man does though. Man says that if God exists, we should be able to understand Him. Man consistently tries to bring God down to man's level. This however merely makes God smaller by removing many of His attributes, and winds up elevating man. If God could be explained and fully understood by finite minds, what kind of God would He be? Certainly not one who would inspire awe.

PLEASE READ THIS UNTIL IT IS UNDERSTOOD
To explain salvation in rational terms then, we could say that God

---

[21] John W. Loftus, *Why I Became an Atheist,* (Amherst: Prometheus Books, 2008), 71

created and when He was done, it was all good. Unfortunately, man fell, introducing evil into this world. Because of that failure, God's laws were broken. God, knowing that the only way man could come back into permanent relationship with Him would be through a sacrifice, insisted that this sacrifice be made because of justice. Because sin creates a debt **to God** as Creator, that debt must be paid. Even if arbitrarily forgiven, the debt would actually still exist.

Man would have to voluntarily sacrifice himself in order to appease God but this would not work because there was not a sinless man to be found ("all have sinned").

Animals could work temporarily, but not permanently because they are not volunteering their lives, nor are they perfect. There was no one individual who was righteous enough (whose value was worth at least as much as all the sin in the world), or perfect enough that could be found who could offer themselves as a sacrifice either for their own sin or anyone else's.

God could not do it as God because He is not human. In order to fully identify with humanity, the sacrifice would need to be fully human, and perfectly sinless.

Why did blood have to spill in order for sin to be cleansed? Because blood goes to the very heart of what makes man tick. To go to that extent by literally giving up all that one possesses (his life) speaks to the complete dedication of that individual. There is no turning back.

But someone else might ask, "Why can't God simply forgive people as people forgive other people?" The answer is that people do *not* forgive people at the level that God forgives. When we forgive another, we are not literally *setting aside* their wrongdoing from a judicial standpoint. We are essentially saying that we will not harbor resentment. We will let it go. We will forego the demand for justice.

If someone attacked and killed my son, and they were found, arrested and convicted of this crime, I would hope to get to a point of being able to truly forgive that person. However, the state would not forgive that person and that individual would be sentenced to either a long prison term, or execution.

Sin Creates Debt Which <u>Must</u> Be Paid
Sin, or wrongdoing, has consequences. Often the consequences (even without punishment) can be severe. Sin creates debt. Even if God were to arbitrarily decide to forgive all sin, the *debt would still exist*. Could God just write it off? No, because that would put things completely out of balance. The debt (or cost of the wrongdoing) needs to be *absorbed* by something or someone. In Matthew 18, we read of the king who *forgave* the debt, by literally absorbing it. The debt simply did not just go away though. It was still there, but the king released the man from *owing* it. In essence then, the king absorbed it by losing the money he was owed. That loss deeply and financially affected that king.

The Stench of Sin
When people sin against God, law is broken and God is highly offended by the stench of it. Sin actually strikes out at God, especially murder because man was made in God's image. Restitution is needed for those broken laws. Even if God chose to say "All is forgiven," the *debt* (the result of that sin) would remain, *unless there was a way for God to absorb it*.

This is exactly what He did through Jesus Christ. God is just and holy. The debt *had to* be paid and could not simply be canceled without payment. Paying the debt meant finding something that was *at least* as valuable as the sum total of the debt in order to be able to pay it off. The substitutionary death of the priceless life of Jesus Christ was the only option.

God, in choosing to be born of a virgin, became clothed in humanity. He then lived a full life of thirty-something years among humanity, completely identifying with them. As God, Christ was unable to sin and as Man, He was able *not* to sin. In essence, every time Jesus was tempted, He took that temptation to its fullest extent, but never gave into it. He passed the test every time and it is because of that sinless life that He *became* the perfect atonement for humanity.

God the Son Paid the Debt
This is exactly WHY Jesus was and remains God. Only God could pay the price and absorb the debt. No one else could have done it. Anyone less than God would not have held up under the full release of God the Father's wrath as He poured it out on His Son as He hung there on Calvary's cross for my sin and yours.

Jesus was born of a woman (while remaining God; flesh merely clothing His deity), lived a sinless life, and offered Himself as propitiation (atonement; payment) for sin. Christ was literally treated by God the Father as though He *was* sin. His righteous wrath was poured out on Jesus Christ, God the Son, as He hung on that cross *instead of upon each human being*, who rightfully deserves His wrath. The debt had been fully paid.

So great was and is Christ's value (because of His deity, His sinless perfection, and His perfect obedience to the Father at every turn), that His voluntary humiliation and death is enough to legally pay for *every single sin produced by each Christian* throughout their entire lives on earth, with more righteousness left over.

Having settled the issue of the outstanding debt created by sin, those who receive Christ as Savior through a spiritual transaction literally have their slates wiped clean. Their *unrighteousness* is replaced by Christ's *perfect righteousness*. In the place of their sin, Christ's righteousness is imputed (applied). No sin is greater than His righteousness. Please get this!!

To receive Jesus as Savior then means to admit and confess to Him that you have sinned. You understand that your sin keeps you away from God and His salvation. You also recognize your total lack of ability to save yourself. It means asking Jesus to extend to you His salvation. It means asking Him to take up residence in your heart and to begin the *process* of being *remade* into His image, or character.

Desiring salvation that only God in Christ provides means to count the cost. We must understand that following Jesus will invite retribution from the spiritual underworld. Satan and his hordes will do what they can to make your life miserable as they did Christ's and millions of other Christians. It is part of the territory and while Satan means it for our harm, God means it for our growth and good, and for His glory. Persecution and trials in this life *promote* the necessary change so that His image is recreated. No Christian can get through this life unscathed.

Has salvation been explained rationally? No. There is no rational explanation for why God would do what He did in Christ, except for the fact that *He loves us as much as He does*. Love is rarely, if ever rational. Love is not understood by reason. It is not a product of evolution. It is only understood in the actions seen in helping others, by relieving their pain and suffering.

This is truly the greatest story that has ever been told. It is the greatest story that has ever been *lived*. Christ is the *epitome* of love for the lost souls of humanity. No human being could make this up! This is perfect truth. It is love that cannot be measured and yet you reject it? *That* is completely and utterly **irrational**.

Oh, How We Suffer from Evil
John brings up the point that "*The Christian theist must not assume*

there is an answer to the problem of evil before approaching the evidence of suffering in our world."[22] The problem of evil is easy to respond to, yet neither John, nor any of his skeptic or atheist friends would appreciate the answer. In spite of John's arbitrarily artificial rules, it should be noted that *the greater the evil, the greater the contrast between evil and good.* No one would know what good actually was without the existence of evil. It would be impossible to know experientially. If it was known at all, it would merely be head knowledge.

Adam chose his path based on free will, according to the Bible. If so, was man able to freely choose to obey God or do his own thing? And in choosing to rebel, was it man or God who created evil? If God *allowed* or *permitted* evil, this does not make Him the *Author* of it, or *responsible* for it. If God chooses to allow evil to exist, so that good may come of it, that is His prerogative and He does not have to answer to finite creatures about it.

Here are some more questions for the Skeptic and Atheist:

1. How did humanity supposedly come up with the system recognized as Christianity, when it flies in the face of logic that a God would Himself die to pay the debt caused by man's sin?
2. If man *did* supposedly come up with this system, how is it that man came up with the idea of God becoming Man, living among us, dying in man's place, and offering salvation to humanity?
3. What other religious system besides Christianity has included anything even remotely similar to it? If man came up with that scenario (and not God), why is not Christianity even *more* appreciated and accepted because it is the only religion in

---

[22] John W. Loftus, *Why I Became an Atheist,* (Amherst: Prometheus Book, 2008), 71

which God makes the demands and *satisfies the demands Himself*?!

John states "*If after having investigated your religious faith with the presumption of skepticism it passes intellectual muster, then you can have your religious faith. It's that simple. If not, abandon it. Any loving God, who requires us to believe correctly, when we have this extremely strong tendency to accept what we were born into, especially if he'll punish us if we end up being wrong, should surely make the correct religious faith pass the outsider test.*"[23]

He continues with "*If your faith doesn't stand after doing this, then the God of your faith is not worthy of being worshiped.*"[24]

John firmly believes he has arrived at the inescapable conclusion that Christians have very few options at their disposal and he seems to maintain that those options are easily shown to go *nowhere*. In truth, all of humanity has only TWO options at their disposal: to receive or reject salvation.

As has been stated, it would be difficult to argue against John's idea that the religion an individual embraces is built largely upon that individual's sociology and culture. This means absolutely nothing since it is clear from Scripture that God calls people *out* of their sociological culture and into the kingdom of heaven. John's argument is cannon fodder. Light it and watch it blow up.

God's Existence (or Not)
John goes into a philosophical discourse on the existence of God (or lack of it as he would say), using the basic philosophical arguments that anyone who has gone to college is familiar with: *the Ontological*,

---

[23] John W. Loftus, *Why I Became an Atheist,* (Amherst: Prometheus Books, 2008), 71
[24] Ibid, 71

the Cosmological, the Teleological, and he also takes some time to step back into history for a visit with Galileo and the process of science and religion over the ages. Yawn.

Before discussing that, it is important to point out that the Bible simply assumes God's existence. It does not attempt to prove it. It takes it for granted. The skeptic though, believes that God should prove His existence, or at least give enough so that His followers can prove it.

This is the nutshell of it...If a Christian states "God exists," the atheist jumps all over the Christian claiming that in order for the Christian to make that statement, they first must *prove it*. Interestingly enough though, if the atheist makes the same type of declarative statement as many of them do with "There is no god," the burden of proof also falls to them because of the nature of the statement.

They are making a declarative statement of *fact*, which assumes that they have investigated every option, crevice and corner of the heavens and of the universe, which allowed them to arrive at the conclusions they present as factual. But in truth, they have not. It is *impossible* to make such a declarative statement as if it was fact, even if it *is* a negative, because it can in no way be verified empirically. Good luck to anyone who wants to try.

From here, John heads into a discussion of *The Strange and Superstitious World of the Bible*. In essence, the idea of a talking donkey (as in the case of Balaam in the Old Testament book of Numbers 22), giants like Goliath, and all the rest are so far-fetched to John that they must of necessity be relegated to the category of superstitious myth. John's conclusions are based on his opinion and they are simply arbitrary.

This comment is erroneous: *"It's very interesting to me that Christians will believe in the miracles recorded in the Bible, simply because they are recorded in the Bible, but if I claimed I saw one of these miracles yesterday, they would not believe me."*[25] Based on what? Was this put to the scientific test? Was this *proven* before making the statement by conducting a worldwide survey of every Christian? It is certainly what the statement implies. A worldwide survey would be the only way anyone could make that statement as fact.

Besides that, has John ever taken the time to talk with Charismatics or Pentecostals on the subject of miracles? It is difficult to believe that no Christian would believe him. True miracles are not unheard of in today's world.

Continuing to read brings out more insight into what skeptics and atheists alike believe about the Bible and Christianity. One such comment is made by someone named Sam Harris. Apparently Sam's misconceptions regarding Christianity are as real as his lack of understanding of human nature in general. He says, *"Tell a devout Christian that his wife is cheating on him, or that frozen yogurt can make a man invisible, and he is likely to require as much evidence as anyone else, and to be persuaded only to the extent that you give it. Tell him that the book he keeps by his bed was written by an invisible deity who will punish him with fire for eternity if he fails to accept its every incredible claim about the universe, and he seems to require no evidence whatsoever."*[26]

One can only hope that Harris is kidding, but the obvious sense is that he is not. It does point to the often held erroneous views of many skeptics and atheists regarding their understanding of Christianity and Christians. Nowhere does the Bible state that the Chris-

---

[25] John W. Loftus, *Why I Became an Atheist,* (Amherst: Prometheus Books, 2008), 125
[26] John W. Loftus, *Why I Became an Atheist,* (Amherst: Prometheus Books, 2008), 125

tian must believe every "incredible claim" or face eternal hell fire. That is patently wrong and ridiculous.

So Many Choices

The *only* way for an individual to reach their chosen destination of hell initially and the Lake of Fire ultimately, is to reject one, and only one, claim: that *Jesus Christ is who He claimed to be and that He died on the cross for humanity's sin*. Reject that and get ready for a very warm eternity.

If I do not believe musical instruments should be used in church and someone else does, the difference does not mean that either or both of us will wind up in hell, unless of course one or both of us is not really a Christian. It does mean we will likely find different churches to attend.

John points out the high number of various denominations. This has been highlighted many times by atheists, skeptics and even Talmudic Jews. The reason there are so many denominations is often due to issues over church government, or worship, or things similar. These are *not* issues upon which a person's salvation is made or broken, but merely issues of likes and dislikes. There is some freedom in many areas of Scripture, wiggle room in other areas and no wiggle room in yet others. It is really no different than a person enjoying jazz, but not opera. That person would not be found taking in an opera at any given time.

The problem with cults (that John, other atheists, and even Talmudic Jews will group together *with* Christianity), is that they differ markedly from orthodox Christianity (what the early church believed). Because of this, they are *separate* from Christianity because they are actually preaching a *different gospel*. Folks like John will group them all together under one roof because it serves their own argument:

"See? Christians can't even get along and agree, so how do we even know what Christianity is all about anyway?"

The main area of disagreement that keeps cults separated from Christianity involves the *deity of Christ*. Cults like Mormonism, Jehovah's Witnesses, etc., do *not* view Jesus Christ as God, the Second Person of the Trinity. While they will quickly agree that He is *divine*, it is only in fleshing out their meaning of divine that one comes to understand they do not accept Jesus as God.

Paul and a number of others who wrote the New Testament under the guidance of the Holy Spirit dealt with these errors early on, and they have always remained with the church. This certainly makes sense because if the Bible is true, meaning that Satan also exists, he would spend most of his time attacking Christianity because he knows that *it is true*. This is really a no-brainer. It is the Parable of the Wheat and Tares being lived out.

John and many individuals he quotes favor the idea that ancient people were not stupid (and one only has to look at all their accomplishments to know that). When it comes to Christians in modern days though, apparently we *are* stupid, very superstitious and even insipid. Ancient people were superstitious, but can be excused because they did not know any better. Christians today have no such excuse because of things like higher thinking and advances in technology. Therefore being a Christian is not only irrational, but is counterproductive to the progression of society.

Biblical Irregularities Built Upon Superstitions
In dealing with the Old Testament, John discusses the Bible's claim that man was made in God's image. However, it is clear from John's loose eisegesis (reading *into* the text, as opposed to exegesis, which is gaining meaning *from* the text), that he really does not understand what he is talking about. In fact, his lack of understanding of Scrip-

ture is clearly seen in these attempts of his in which he tries to show problems in the text, or contradictory aspects of the Bible in general.

Since he has already removed the supernatural element from the Bible, what he has left to work with is simply a book written by over 40 authors, spanning a 1400 year time period. Even in going to the original Hebrew to discover definitions of words as he does amounts to nothing. Knowing the definition of a word is only part of it. Context is another part. History and culture are yet another part. It would be easy to go to the dictionary and look up the word "left" and find numerous definitions. Which one is the one being used? It depends upon the context and the history and culture.

John declares the theist must not use the Bible to prove that the Bible is true. In other words, no part of the Bible is allowed to speak to any other part of the Bible for any type of corroboration. Why would this be a problem to John? If the supernatural element has been removed by him, and the Christian can still show the remarkable consistency of it even though written by over 40 authors, over a 1400 year period, that *alone* would go quite far in proving its integrity. What other possible work of antiquity claims to have been written by over 40 people, over a period of 1400 years or so? Not one.

John sees no problem in picking the Bible apart at will to support his own incorrect assertions. This is seen time and time again throughout John's book. Muslims, Jews, members of cults and others do this all the time thinking they are onto something. But if the Bible is ultimately God's Word, then it must be allowed to interpret itself. It is disingenuous to go to the Bible (the Christian's book), and demand that it be interpreted only with the rules given by an atheist. Is that rational?

Getting back to the "man made in God's image" concept, God the Father is invisible, yet the God who walked with Adam in the garden and makes appearances in the Old Testament. It is most likely Jesus as Pre-incarnate God the Son. John attempts to downplay these "theophanies" but comes up lacking.

When the Bible speaks of God making man in His image, the Hebrew can refer to physical aspects of the human being, as John points out. It *can* but in this case it does *not*. The sense in which man was created in God's image is in the *spiritual aspect* of humanity This is clear from the *context* since God does not necessarily have a body (unless He chooses to be seen of His creation). This would include the ability to think or reason (as opposed to using merely instinct), resolve problems, use intuition, house a soul, and many other attributes not shared by the animal kingdom. God's creation of man after His image denotes that man has a moral fiber built in, unlike any and all animals.

What does the phrase mean when God is said to have "*breathed into his nostrils the breath of life, and the man became a living creature*" (Genesis 2:7b)? Does it not imply something more than merely making something? Does it not imply something unique and special? When God breathed into man, that act provided man with much more than simply "breath." He became a living creature, and some translations use the term "soul" instead of creature. Man had been created in God's image and the entire Godhead was involved in that process ("Let *us* make man..."). This is why murder is actually striking out at God, and why God instituted the death penalty in Genesis chapter nine.

Note that prior to this all creatures were made *after their own kind*, but not man. Man was made in God's image. This speaks of the supreme importance and value of man with the scope of God's full creation. Both evolutionists and atheists alike downplay the value and worth of humanity.

God Has Arms

God was often seen in the pillar of fire or the cloud, or in other ways that the people could *comprehend* and that would allow them to connect with because they could see it. But John has a reason for not accepting these theophanies: it is because he believes Christians approach Scripture understanding it in terms that were applied to these passages *later* on by other believers. Really. So, later on it was Christians who decided that the Pillar of Fire was really God, or the glory shown round about the Ark of the Covenant was really the Shechinah Glory? So, the Jews themselves never saw it like this, is that correct? Wrong.

The fact that it is believed that Jesus is viewed as the "Angel of the LORD" for instance, has much more to do with the textual meaning of Scripture than anything else.

But let us take a moment to look at John's "reasoning" here. It is agreed that Jesus as Jesus did not exist in the Old Testament. The Godhead did exist of course, but Jesus had not physically been born of the virgin Mary yet. God was God and though there is enough reference to prove the Trinity from the Old Testament, Jesus was not yet in view.

After Jesus was born and lived on this earth, He began saying things and teaching things that connected Himself with the Old Testament ("Before Abraham was, I AM", etc.). So Who was it that actually made the connection? Jesus Christ made the connection. Christians did not "figure this out" later on. They heard it from the God-Man Himself.

One by one, John goes through the biblical text, pointing out claims from the Bible, and dismissing them because there is no accompanying proof of any kind outside of the Bible. His one main assertion is that everything within the Old Testament can be explained by understanding that the people of Israel were superstitious. Whether it was

Daniel determining the meaning of Nebuchadnezzar's dream or Jonah being swallowed by a "large fish," or manna falling from heaven, or whatever, it can all be explained based on the superstitious beliefs of the time. But again, John is simply viewing Scripture through his own particular template and offering nothing conclusive as direct proof of his claims, and his circumstantial evidence is no proof at all. He is simply rewriting Scripture to suit himself.

Bereft of the Supernatural
John removes the supernatural element then wonders what would happen if any of these things took place today. How would people react to them? This is absurd, because he would first rewrite those events so that they did not even appear to be miraculous. The parting of the Red (Reed) Sea would be Moses wading out into eight inches of swamp water and using a shovel to divert the water!

This is what he has attempted to do throughout his book. John fails to understand the biblical reasons for instance, for why there was so much killing in the Old Testament, or why God chose people like Moses or Elijah to speak through, or why Jesus healed people, or why Jesus cast out demons *from the person who could not speak.* John proves over and over again that he has absolutely no clue.

One can only wonder what type of preacher he was when he considered himself to be a Christian. Far from trying to be insulting, the question must be asked…what *did* he preach on? What was his view of Scripture *then* as a "Christian"? Did he believe the miracles as miracles then? How about Soteriology, or Eschatology, or Angelology, or Hamartiology, etc.?

John, along with higher critics, claim the Bible was not really written when it is supposed to have been written, and that certain books were not really written by the individuals credited with writing them. While he points to others who support this viewpoint, he offers no proof of those claims, or proof that the Bible is wrong. John has merely traded his belief in the Bible for belief in the opinions of other atheists, who along with himself, are his current and highest authority.

By eliminating the spiritual or supernatural from Scripture, those passages considered to be too difficult to believe become clearly questionable simply because they are not natural events. In order to make them natural events, John and others have to rewrite the Bible, question the integrity of people and even label them liars. This he does with no proof, but merely conjecture and because it seems reasonable to do so, since the miracles could not really have occurred as recorded in Scripture. So much for research and journalistic integrity. The assaults on the text of Scripture are easily answered, but will John or any other atheist be convinced with these answers? Of course not, because they fall back on the *"I've got to see it, or see proof of it before I can accept it"* statement as their failsafe. Yet they believe in evolution with no proof, but merely working hypotheses.

John Interprets

For example, in dealing with several instances in the book of Acts where we learn of Paul's (and Barnabas') situation in Lystra, John finds it difficult to believe Luke's account of the miracle of the lame man being healed. *"I know that this is difficult to dispute, since the story is written by Luke...what I do know is that such things are claimed by Benny Hinn's followers all of the time, as well as Oral Roberts. I also know that Luke was a believer and he wanted to tell a story that would cause other people to believe."*[27]

This argument has absolutely no merit, unless a smoke screen is considered to be meritorious. A smoke screen. That is all this is. Benny

---

[27] John W. Loftus, *Why I Became an Atheist,* (Amherst: Prometheus Books, 2008), 154-55

Hinn and Oral Roberts are liars. How does this prove that *Luke* lied? How does this prove that the narrative of Jesus was *falsely* reported by His disciples? John's argument also presupposes that Luke *knew* that he was writing accounts that would be read by millions of people, when in point of fact, the Scriptures indicate that he wrote both the gospel of Luke and the book of Acts for only *one other person*: *Theophilus* (cf. Acts 1:1). How is it that Luke told a story "that would cause others to believe" if there had been no real thought about putting his work on the Ancient Jerusalem Times bestseller list? It is obvious that he was writing personal correspondence. Once again John's argument falls completely flat.

Beyond this, there is no connection of Paul with Benny Hinn, or Oral Roberts, or Kathryn Kuhlman, or any other individual who claims to be a "faith healer."

For one thing, there is no such thing as the position of faith healer in Scripture. Those who were able to heal (through prayer and the empowering of the Holy Spirit) as part of their ministry did not see this as their *main* vocation or gift. Their main responsibility was evangelizing. Often God provided the ability to perform the miraculous because it *verified* the message and the messenger.

As John himself would say, there was a great deal of divination and magic during those days based on superstitions of the times. God's miracles had to be real, effective, and something that could not be replicated. John also says that the people were not stupid. It is obvious they would have instantly known the difference between a charlatan magician and the real deal, as in the case of Jesus' miracles or the ones done through Paul, or Peter, vs. Simon the Sorcerer (read about Simon in Acts 8).

Liar, Liar, Pants on Fire
John finished his critique by stating "*I require more evidence to be-*

lieve something like this than a mere report by someone in the past who lived and breathed among people who were wildly superstitious."[28] So did "doubting" Thomas. John's statement at first glance appears intelligent, but is actually a statement devoid of it. He has already shown us that his powers of deduction are severely lacking, making mistakes in interpretation that are easily avoided. He has shown us that his first approach to something like this is to automatically doubt its legitimacy.

It would actually serve his purposes far better if he were to attempt to *prove* the veracity of events like these, as opposed to always assuming they could not have occurred.

As it stands now, he not only doubts everything, but merely winds up rewriting it to his liking. How is that even remotely scientific? Would it not be better to at least attempt to show impartiality by finding ways these situations may have occurred exactly as written, yet naturally as opposed to supernaturally? While he attempts to do this with some of the events he discusses, by and large, he rewrites instead of explains how events may have happened naturally.

A skeptic is in the best possible place, at least as far as this type of research and experimentation is concerned. A true skeptic, far from wishing to *disprove* that something occurred as reported, will do what they can to show that there is a *natural explanation* for it happening the way it was described.

The skeptic can truly approach the situation seeking to provide a natural cause for the event *exactly as it happened*. John does not do that. He merely rewrites the events because they do not make sense to him otherwise. He is convinced that they could not have happened

---

[28] John W. Loftus, *Why I Became an Atheist,* (Amherst: Prometheus Books, 2008), 154

the way they are reported, so he changes them by rewriting them so that they are now believable to him. But this proves absolutely nothing.

The True Skeptic
James Randi is a skeptic who has taken it upon himself to debunk magicians, psychics and those of that genre. He is very good at what he does.

On one show he was on, a number of supposed psychics came to prove that the psychic world exists. One particular gentlemen came on the show and said he could, by just using psychic ability, turn the pages of the phone book. While he did this, Randi stood to the side watching patiently and intently.

Sure enough, after one false start, this psychic was able to get the pages to turn. There was applause and cheers. The host asked Randi if there was something other than psychic powers that caused the pages to turn. Without hesitating, Randi said there was, and to prove it he would like the psychic to do the trick again, but this time with Styrofoam™ peanuts near the phone book as he used his psychic powers.

The psychic said he could not do it all the time, because it depended largely on the psychic world. Ultimately he refused, so Randi did the trick and it was impressive. Randi showed how the man – as he waved his hands gently over the open phone book to create a diversion – actually used his breath to blow the pages, so that it looked like the pages were being turned with psychic powers. He then did it with the peanuts to prove that breath was being used.

In this case, Randi did not *rewrite* the trick. He did not change it in any way, shape, or form. He allowed the "psychic" to do the trick as he normally did it, then simply asked him to put something near the trick, to act as a monitor. It would not affect it if in fact it was really done with psychic powers.

James Randi is someone who is an honest to goodness skeptic because he explains how something happens, *without changing the actual event*. John Loftus does not do this. He approaches the event with doubt (just like Randi), but unlike Randi, he changes the event, seemingly refusing to even consider that there might be a completely natural explanation for these events.

While he states that he believes nearly every supposed supernatural event can be explained naturally, he seems not to believe his own words. If someone is going to say that they believe nearly all supernatural events can be explained naturally, then the obligation is to recreate the event exactly like the first one, except recreate it using natural methods, as opposed to supernatural. John simply replaces the original event that is difficult to believe with one that is very easy for him to believe. He has proven nothing though, except that he can rewrite events and doubt they occurred as noted. Whoopee.

There are some great magicians today who *seem* to be able to do things that are supernatural. They are not, and when it is discovered how the tricks are done, people will react with, "Oh man, *that's* how it's done?" People can be fooled and often are, but they are also smart enough to figure things out.

Another question for John is this: what evidence does he think could be used to prove the event took place? In truth, there could be *no* evidence that would be good enough simply because there is nothing outside the Bible that can corroborate this incident, or many others. Who would write about it? The people of Lystra? Even if they did, would their account be believed any more than Luke's narrative? Of course not. There is nothing that can be entered into evidence in a court of law that would *prove* beyond doubt that this event happened. Nothing. Even if they had a way to video tape the event or snap photos of it, John would not be convinced, because these things can be doctored. There really is nothing that would convince John that this event happened as recorded. It is doubtful that even if a miracle was done in front of John, with him seeing it, he would believe it even then. John is actually worse than a skeptic. He has become a man who is utterly *unable to be convinced.*

If John could recreate any of the events in the Bible to look as they are described, then he might have a case that he could build on to prove that God does not exist and Christianity is a sham. Why? Because he is able to replicate them, using natural means. Until then, he really has nothing and offers us the same in his book.

Searching and Not Finding
But John continues looking for more clues to determine whether it could have taken place. He brings up the fact that Paul mainly spoke to the common people and then states *"we are hardly ever talking about the educated classes in the New Testament. It's almost always, unless specified, the common average classes or lower classes that Jesus and Paul reached. And so far, those classes of people seemed overwhelmingly superstitious."*[29] It is good that he said "almost" and "hardly ever" because there were several situations in Acts when Paul spoke before governors and kings. They reacted no differently than these "common folk." John also forgets that Paul always went to synagogues in a new city or town first. Synagogues were usually filled with men who had a decent education.

John also seems to be forgetting the type of individual Jesus hung around with (the sinners, publicans, and tax collectors). He was roundly criticized for doing so, but His answer tells everything that

---

[29] John W. Loftus, *Why I Became an Atheist,* (Amherst: Prometheus Books, 2008), 155

anyone needs to know: *"Those who are well have no need of a physician, but those who are sick."* (Matthew 9:12)

Jesus daily dealt with the needs of the common person, as well as the Scribes and Pharisees. Yet, as John has pointed out, these common people were not stupid, just superstitious. They obviously understood points being made by Jesus. Moreover, they were impressed with the fact that He came across as having more authority than the religious leaders of that time (cf. John 7:46; Matthew 7:29, etc.).

Nonetheless John's statement about the common person implies that upper class people then were *not* generally superstitious and this is easily disproven. *All classes of* people of the ancient world were superstitious, just as all classes of people in this modern world of ours are superstitious. It was not solely the common or lower class people who worshiped in the temples. Kings and queens were no exception to superstitions and had their entire group of advisors, which were largely made up of diviners, magicians and sorcerers. Remember Nebuchadnezzar? To say that it was only the common person who was superstitious is patently wrong. John agrees that the kings and queens and others who governed were superstitious, but he excuses them by stating that they were really only doing that for political purposes and did not really believe the superstitions. This again is patently wrong. Many rulers and important people of the ancient world were extremely superstitious. How about Constantine and his "by this sign conquer," after stating that he saw a cross in the sky and believed it to be a sign from God? From here, he went on a murdering spree and God got the blame.

Do the lives of more people need to be recounted here in order to prove that? The facts are available for anyone who is seriously interested in knowing the truth about history.

His doubts prove nothing; nothing at all. Yet he presents them as if he has uncovered the Ark of the Covenant. It is too bad there is not space enough to deal with each of Mr. Loftus' claims regarding the Bible and his "contradictions." Even if there was enough space here, it would be way too tedious to do so. He finds things "strange" that are really not strange at all, and finds the normal, abnormal.

Confusing?
On one hand John states that the people *then* were really superstitious, which is the main reason they chose to view Paul and Barnabas as gods. Yet even though the people obviously got caught up in the frenzy of worshiping them (and were deaf to Paul's protestations because of it), John finds fault with the fact that they did not listen to Paul or Barnabas when they tried to tell that them they were not gods.

John finds this strange, yet if these people were so superstitious (and this is not denied), then it *would* be strange that they *would stop their attempts to worship* in favor of having a chat with two gods! If they were gods, you worship them first so that they do not kill you now! It was *because* of their superstitions that they immediately began to worship, for *not* to worship was potentially to invite that gods' wrath. It simply took Paul a few minutes to get their attention and get them to hear him. That is all there was to it.

John also has a difficulty with the next paragraph which states that the Jews "won the crowd over" after listening to Paul. He argues that those in the crowd who were largely polytheistic would not have listened to the Jews, who were monotheistic. He winds up proving again that he has no clue about that which he speaks by merely presenting his opinion as if it is a foregone conclusion.

Even if his assertion was true (which it is not), John misses the point Luke is making here. The Jews, though not well-liked by the majority of people, certainly would have been *deferred to* by these superstitious people, if for no other reason than because of the God "the Jews" represented.

Whenever the Bible uses the phrase "the Jews" it is usually referring to the Jewish religious leaders of the day; part of the Sanhedrin. They commanded respect by everyone. Whether they were *liked* was another matter altogether, but they commanded respect, just like many emperors who were despised by people, yet obeyed. Why? Because they held the power of death. The Jews could easily set you up as a blasphemer or traitor against Rome and there would be little you could do about it once their political machine started working.

Sad You See
The Sadducees were the atheists of their day. They believed in no afterlife at all, and being the religious leaders of the Jews was merely a political position that came with a great deal of power and prestige. It was a highly sought after position by many. If you had enough money and proper connections, you could easily buy your way into becoming one of the Sadducees.

John finds the fact that they stoned Paul to be incredulous. He says *"The only reason they might have listened to what the Jews said is that they claimed Paul and Barnabas were demons or demon possessed. "But Paul and Barnabas would be right there denying it. So whom would you believe?"*[30]

Stoning someone because they were demon-possessed? That is not a crime punishable by death. It is not even a crime. In fact, this author cannot off hand recall one event in the Bible where a person who was demon-possessed was stoned to death. But John is also assuming (at

---

[30] John W. Loftus, *Why I Became an Atheist,* (Amherst: Prometheus Books, 2008), 155

least in this instance) that there is perfect justice in the world, yet he argues in his book that in the world, the problem of evil does not exist.

Apparently John has also forgotten his own situations in life; the ones that caused him to reject Christianity. One need only refer to John's own circumstances in which he was *not* believed by everyone, yet there he was standing there, telling them the truth. Is that not used as at least one reason why he left the faith? In spite of that, he presupposes that this same thing would *not* have occurred with Paul and Barnabas and that they would have been immediately believed. Why does he assume this? He offers no real proof that they would have been believed, but simply jumps to that conclusion. It is faulty reasoning at best. This is simply another contradiction in a long line of contradictory words and thoughts from John W. Loftus, ex-Christian. Paul was stoned and left for dead. He did not give up on Christ. John Loftus was *not* stoned or left for dead. He *did* give up on Christ.

One further point on this. If we look at the text closely (Acts 14:8-21), it says *"But Jews came from Antioch and Iconium, and having won over the crowd, they stoned Paul and dragged him out of city, supposing him to be dead"* (Acts 14:19), we see something interesting. The Jews successfully "won over the crowd" by likely reporting to them what Paul and Barnabas had done in *previous* cities. These Jews had been "chasing after Paul and Barnabas, following them from city to city denouncing them in each place," they would tell the crowd. Looking at the first few verses of Acts 14 confirms that these same Jews "stirred up" that crowd in Iconium. Notice that there was also an attempt to stone Paul and Barnabas while there.

If we consider what took place prior to that in chapter thirteen of Acts, at Antioch, we have a situation which is also similar. The Jews stirred up the crowds by accusing Paul and Barnabas of blasphemy. This crime *is* punishable by death (stoning) in Judaism. The crowds of Jews and "devout women" (Gentile proselytes to Judaism; cf. v. 43), literally drove them out of the city of Antioch there, though.

The reality is that if the Jews could get the crowd to believe that Paul and Barnabas were guilty of blasphemy (not demon-possession), that would have been enough to stone them. Any other Jews in that city would have joined in the stoning process. It is really quite simple, as has been shown, and is not as incredulous to believe as John implies.

Which Is It?
At one point, John is claiming the ancient people are extremely superstitious and then at another point, he is claiming that they would have been sensible. Cheese and crackers, his naiveté is obviously ambiguous. It cannot be both ways, yet apparently John thinks that it can be.

The reality though (again) is that he has removed any semblance of supernatural from the Bible. Far from being able to judge the Bible rationally through reason as he believes he is doing, he has simply set himself up as *god* in authoritatively reviewing and denouncing the Bible as something filled with unbelievable scenarios. If you take away the supernatural, of *course* they are unbelievable scenarios.

Again, it has to be asked, what human being (or over 40 human beings, stretched across 1400 years) would come up with something as is presented to us in the Bible, especially as it concerns redemption and salvation? While there is no disagreement with the fact that Paul often witnessed to and evangelized superstitious people, it does not follow that because they were superstitious, they were stupid (and even John stated this in his book). Since they were not stupid, it *should* stand to reason that they were capable of *learning and understanding*.

The gospel of Jesus Christ as it goes throughout the world has been and will be met with all types of resistance. This was shown to be fact in the Bible and it is fact today since Christ's day.

If the Bible is at all real, that means that Christ is real, and Satan is real. It stands to reason that *if* Christianity is the only way that offers true salvation, would not Satan use every ounce of strength within him to fight against that system? Would he not do this to keep people from gaining that salvation? That i*s absolutely rational, making perfect sense.*

John's Anti-Supernatural Bias

But the real difficulty lies in the fact as John has stated, that he has an *anti-supernatural bias* (which is where the title of this book came from). This bias of his keeps him from even *entertaining* the idea that things which occurred in the Bible could have occurred as reported.

John constantly states that Paul is wrong in this idea or that, yet again offers no proof of it. What he is really doing is simply providing his *opinion* about the accuracy of Paul (with respect to idol worship in Acts, for instance), which simply comes off as arrogance on John's part. Paul did not misunderstand the nature of idols as John insists. While those images created by human beings represented the gods (and were *not* the actual gods), they were so closely connected to their particular deity that to damage the idol was akin to an assault on the deity. Paul knew what he was talking about. Moreover, he put things in the terminology that the people would understand because of their superstitions.

John next deals with the situation in Athens (Acts 17:16ff). He has another problem with the use of the term "reasoned" referencing Paul and his discussion with the Jews and the God-fearing Greeks in the marketplace. John believes that whoever wrote the narrative used the word "reasoned" to support his own belief that Paul's reasoning was *better* than that of his hearers. This is *not* what the text states or means. A better rendition of the Greek word here might have been "debating," because that is what reasoning is referring to here; a *give and take; a discussion and <u>exchange</u> of ideas.*

The market place was where the open exchange of ideas was the norm. This is exactly what Paul did. He was exchanging ideas; debating with people about their idol worship and the one, true God. Luke (though not there at the time of the incident), is *not* stating that Paul's reasoning was better than anyone else's. It simply means that he *presented* his understanding of the Law and Prophets as they related to Christ.

This would be no different than going to any college in the United States that has a free speech area. In that area, a person can speak about whatever he wants to speak about and *reason* with the crowd. Does that mean that no one is going to disagree with that person, or will not *reason* back at him? Of course not, but because the person speaking to the crowd is the focus, it is he who is doing the reasoning. It is really very simple.

In that same instance, John has a problem with the phrase "all the Athenians" because he says that this is inaccurate and an outright lie to use the word "all."

Here is the text from Acts 17:21, *"(Now all the Athenians and the strangers visiting there used to spend their time in nothing other than telling or hearing something new.)"*

He then gives an example from a newspaper in which they might print "All the people in..." leading one to believe that every single person from a city was involved. This of course is viewed as duplicitous by John, and he is not the first person to make such a ridiculous charge against the veracity of the Bible.

Does it not appear as though Luke is simply making generalizations to make a point? He does not mean "all" anymore than he means that those people did nothing but telling or hearing something new.

Everybody Cheered!
John has apparently never attended or read about a sporting event in which it was reported that at the winning goal, *the crowd was on their feet*, or *all stood* cheering, whistling and screaming. What if there were one or two or ten people who did not stand up, but remained sitting in their seats clapping and screaming their brains out? (By the way, if one were to use the phrase "screaming their brains out," would that mean that they were screaming so long and loud that their brains really popped out of their heads?)

What if some in attendance were in wheelchairs and unable to stand up, yet they were just as involved in the celebration? What if some did not whistle, but clapped only? Would the news reporter be accused of lying? This type of hyper-literalistic reading *into* the text when it comes to Scripture is completely artificial and goes against logic. *It is not rational.* No one with any semblance of intelligence while reading the Scripture (or any other written literature) takes phrases like that *hyper-literally* when they are obviously not meant that way. It is this type of errant thinking that leads John to state *"Since we know this report in Acts is a gross exaggeration..."*[31] Actually, John *believes* and has *decided* it to be a gross exaggeration. He does not know it, nor can he prove it, and his attempts at doing so fall flat, except possibly to other atheists and skeptics.

The passage does actually say "*All the Athenians...*" It also says they spent "*their time in nothing other than telling...*" Apparently, John has no difficulty with this phrase. This is what is called in literary terms,

---

[31] John W. Loftus, *Why I Became an Atheist,* (Amherst: Prometheus Books, 2008), 156

a *hyperbole*, and it is used to make a point. If all these folks did was debate, can we assume then that they never went to the bathroom? Never bought or sold goods? Never ate anything? Never did anything except debate? This is obviously not what was meant. The question must be asked: *who really takes language in this manner?*

"Man, that's all he ever does is sit around picking his nose" is an example of the type of figurative hyperbole that people use to point out the abject laziness of someone. It is not taken *hyper-literally;* no one would think that person actually did that. The literal **meaning** as we know is *"That guy is completely lazy."* Who actually sits around doing nothing for 24 hours each day except pick his nose? This is an exaggeration; not a lie. The Bible is filled with figurative and poetic language, as well as euphemisms and other forms of expressive language. They are often used to make a point.

Chapter 6

A Bite in Malta

(and other seeming dilemmas)

In another instance John highlights Paul's arrival on the island of Malta where he is promptly bitten by a snake. The text says *"a viper, driven out by the heat, fastened itself on his hand."* (Acts 28)

John comments *"I don't think the incident occurred as reported. 'Fastened on his hand'; later he 'shook it off.' Most snakebites are very quick. And if it was quick, maybe the venom wasn't enough to kill or even hurt Paul?*"[32] Here John opts for rewriting the text based on his understanding of snake bites. Is he correct? Does he offer anything substantial to back up his claim, or is he simply rewriting the text to make it sound much less *supernatural* (since we know he simply discounts the supernatural as invalid)?

Most, If, Maybe...Huh?
Please note that in his objections to Dr. Luke's narrative, John uses the words "most," "if," "maybe," and says "*Most snakebites are very quick.*" He sounds a bit unsure. Nonetheless he makes that statement, but offers nothing substantial as *proof* that his statements are correct and Luke's are incorrect, or even that his own statements *could* have merit at all. John is doing exactly what he says he cannot accept from many of the biblical writers; making statements with no proof attached. There is nothing *empirical* about John's assessments.

John says "Most snakebites are very quick." However, he proceeds as if he has actually used the word "all," as in "All snakebites are very quick." Does anyone else notice the duplicity here? He says *one thing*, but in reality *means another*. He says "most" but means "all" or at least hopes that the reader *thinks* he used "all."

John apparently believes that merely voicing his objection to Luke's account proves beyond doubt that his difficulty with the passage is correct. Paul could have only been bitten by a snake that strikes its victim quickly and recoils just as quickly. There is no other option, John implies. He does toss in the other possibility of a low amount of venom as a caveat, in case any doubts remain about his first assertion. He assumes that we are right there with him. It is a slam dunk. Case closed.

---

[32] John W. Loftus, *Why I Became an Atheist,* (Amherst: Prometheus Books, 2008), 159

Let us recall John's own words: *"I require more evidence to believe something like this than a mere report by someone in the past who lived and breathed among people who were wildly superstitious."* Based on that, should we not expect him to provide infallible proof that his assertions which contradict the report given in Acts are the correct assertions and the ones in Acts false? That would certainly be rational. It follows then that short of providing proof, John is merely providing an *opinion* which bears no weight at all.

In fact, if it can be *proven* that John's inference regarding snakebites is utterly false, then the narrative in Acts *must stand as it is written*.

It must be ascertained if John has actually *proven* anything that would allow us to *agree* with him. John has <u>said</u> "most snakebites," but appears to <u>mean</u> "all snakebites." If he does not mean "all snakebites," he has no reason to disagree with the narrative. Hence, he has no rational reason to reject the Acts narrative as it currently reads.

While we know that certain snakes *do* bite and release quickly, we also know from researching the subject that other snakes do <u>not</u>.

"Copperheads, bushmasters, and other vipers inject their venom and then release the prey immediately, later following the scent trail to find the dead animal. Others, such as **cobras, simply hang onto the prey they have poisoned and swallow it when its struggles have ceased***"*[33] (emphasis mine).

Another article states *"Elapids generally have short fangs. When elapids bite,* **they usually hang onto their prey***. This gives their poison-*

---

[33] http://encarta.msn.com/encnet/refpages/RefArticle.aspx?refid=761578341&pn=3

ous venom more of a chance to enter the victim's body"[34] (emphasis mine). Elapids are a type of *viper*, interestingly enough.

In yet another online source we read, *"Proteroglyphous snakes **typically bite and hold their prey**, and then chew to inject venom deep in the wound. This behaviour is virtually universal among sea snakes, whose fish prey would otherwise swim or drift away before being incapacitated (by) an envenomating strike-bite and withdraw"*[35] (emphasis mine).

And another site states, *"Black mambas usually bite their prey once or twice and then allow it go off to die before attempting to eat. They may however, **bite and hold when eating birds**"*[36] (emphasis mine).

Now if this author can spend less than ten minutes searching for this information, why could John not have done the same? Would that not have been the *reasonable* and logical thing to do?

Venomous vs. Non-Venomous
One individual commenting on this particular situation described by Luke says, *"Some commentators have gone so far as to suggest that this viper was not venomous at all, based upon the fact that such snakes no longer are found on Malta—no great surprise for a small island, quite well populated. They would have us believe that both these 'primitives' and Luke were in error. This is incredible, on both counts. First, Luke was writing under inspiration, in the power and guidance of the Holy Spirit. He could not have erred. In addition, Luke was a doctor, who may well have treated a number of snake bite wounds already. Doctors are not careless about the identification of snakes which might have a fatal bite.*

---

[34] http://animals.howstuffworks.com/snakes/snake-info.htm
[35] http://www.reptileallsorts.com/bites-venom.htm
[36] http://www.kingsnake.com/elapids/black_mamba.htm

"These 'primitives' (as some would refer to them) were far more knowledgeable about snakes than those 'experts' who would tell us that the creature that bit Paul was a non-poisonous snake. The natives who live and work in an area which has poisonous snakes know their snakes well. They don't make mistakes about such matters. Their life depends upon it. In India and Africa, as well as in rural areas in the Southwest, the 'natives' know their snakes. So too, with the natives on Malta. The snake fastened itself on Paul's hand. It did not strike, as a rattler would do. It clung, something like a coral snake. They knew what kind of snake the creature was, and what happened when it bit someone. They waited for a sequence of events they had seen too many times before. They waited for Paul's hand to swell up, and then for him to die. This is what would have happened, without divine intervention.

"God did intervene. Paul seemed to go on as usual, and time passed. It eventually became clear that Paul was not going to die, or even to be affected in any way by the snake bite."[37]

And by the way, the word translated "primitives" actually means simply "islanders," which provides a completely different mental picture than the word "primitives."

Beyond this, one might go an additional step to cover all the bases, and ask if any such snakes even existed on the island of Malta during Paul's time.

"Today there are no vipers indigenous to Malta. Great changes have taken place since the first century C.E. Whereas now Malta is one of the most densely populated islands in the world, with about 1,280 persons per sq km (3,330 per sq mi); extensive wooded areas may have existed there in Paul's time. The population increase would have had a marked effect on the habitats of wildlife. This could easily have caused all vi-

---

[37] http://www.bible.org/page.php?page_id=2161

pers to disappear, as was the case in Arran, an island off the SW coast of Scotland. As late as 1853, however, a viper is reported to have been seen near St. Paul's Bay."[38]

It is clear then that what Dr. Luke described could very well have occurred and likely did. So what have we learned? We have learned that John jumps to conclusions (which is not rational), in an effort to sustain his own presuppositions and in doing so, does a terrible job of supporting those conclusions. Not only has John *not* proven his assertions, or implications, but it has been proven that the actual narrative found in the book of Acts is likely to be truthful and needs no adjustment.

Proving the Supernatural, Naturally

For the sake of philosophical argument, IF the narrative happened as it did in the book of Acts, then there would be only one way to see it as a *natural event* (as opposed to a supernatural event), which would still require proof: *The event happened as written, with Paul being bitten. The venom did nothing to Paul because he had been bitten so many times before by this type of snake that he had developed a natural immunity to it.*

That is an example of *explaining the supernatural with the natural*. No need for rewrites. Simply do not disclose everything to the audience. However, **as stated**, rather than simply *adopting* this scenario because it sounds good to the atheist, it still must be *proven* that this is exactly what happened; that some aspect of truth was suppressed in order to create faith in the supernatural.

To prove this, the researcher would need to find evidence of:

- Paul being bitten by this type of snake before;

---

[38] http://wiki.answers.com/Q/Were_there_venomous_snakes_in_Malta_during_the_time_of_Acts_28_verses_3-6

- Paul traveling to Malta before;
- If he'd been to Malta before, how many times?
- Snakes like the ones existing in other areas of the then known world;
- Exactly *which* type of snake lived on Malta during the time of Paul's visit?
- The veracity of Luke. Can it be proven that he was given to lying?

If it can be proven that Paul, throughout his life, had been the victim of many snake bites, then a natural explanation for this event *might* have some merit. Short of being able to do all of the above and more, the narrative must stand as written.

It becomes embarrassingly obvious that John is doing his level best to tear down Scripture, but he simply does not have the proper tools for the job. His methods are certainly questionable at best.

Mr. JEPD
Reading through the remainder of John's book brings us into contact with many other alleged contradictions that have surfaced over the years, such as, if Moses died at the end of Deuteronomy, how could Moses have written the end of the book? It is safe to say that Moses wrote all of Deuteronomy except the part after his death, unless of course God revealed to Moses when he would die and what would happen afterwards.

It is plain that someone else penned the last bit of the book. Duh. This neither negates the inspiration of that book, or any aspect of Scripture.

People still continue to cling to the Documentary Hypothesis, otherwise known as the Graf-Wellhausen Theory (or the JEPD theory), which claims that aspects of the first five books of the Bible were not written by Moses, but by several different authors. This view, in spite of being debunked years ago, is still something that atheists continue to cling to because in believing it (regardless of evidence or proof to the contrary), they can continue to maintain that the supernatural aspect of the Bible is gone. If the supernatural element is gone, so too is God and His authority. This is what 'higher critics' attempt to do, but goodness only knows why they are referred to as *higher* critics.

John talks about a "very serious" problem with Jeremiah 7:22, though it is really difficult to believe that John is actually serious with many of these "problems" he points out. It is terrible to burst someone's bubble, but there is *no* problem in this text, much less a very serious one. It is a problem for those liberal theologians, atheists and higher critics who believe that this text teaches that Israel was promised the land but did not get it. There is no way that all aspects of this text can be covered here. However, in an upcoming book (*When the Rightful Owner Returns*), this author will cover all major aspects of properly interpreting sections of Scripture related to Eschatology.

John makes outlandish statements like, "*It has long been accepted that the present book of Isaiah was compiled by at least two authors, and probably three.*"[39] Really? That *is* interesting, and indeed news to this author. Searching commentary after commentary underscored the exact *opposite*; that Isaiah came down through the ages as a unit and this Isaiah was the son of Amoz. In fact, one source states this: "*Until late in the eighteenth century, only one extant writer questioned the universal assumption that Isaiah wrote the whole book, namely the twelfth-century Jewish commentator Ibn Ezra.*"[40]

Dig This
John also tries his hand digging through the archaeological record to

---

[39] John W. Loftus, *Why I Became an Atheist,* (Amherst: Prometheus Books, 2008), 169
[40] Geoffry W. Grogan, *The Expositor's Bible Commentary,* (Grand Rapids: Zondervan), 6

highlight what he believes is a complete lack of evidence related to the Exodus and the Canaanite Conquest. This is unfortunately a commonly accepted *misconception* among atheists. Rather than repeat what others have researched and written, it will suffice here simply to list a few sources that provide some excellent insight into many of the archaeological discoveries that have been uncovered related to the Exodus and other aspects of the Torah:

- http://ohr.edu/ask/ask158.htm#Q1
- http://ohr.edu/yhiy/article.php/838 (Ipuwer papyrus)
- *Israel in Egypt* by James Hoffmeier
- *Biblical Personalities and Archaeology* by Leah Bronner
- *Permission to Receive* by Leib Keleman

Now, why was John not able to locate any information on the Exodus within the realm of archaeology? Maybe he was not really looking. He is already convinced that he is right and Christianity is wrong.

We have included in the last chapter of this book, some information regarding the Exodus and evidence for it, but the previously highlighted sources will give much more detail and a more complete picture.

John also takes on the Holy Spirit and His "self-authenticating" witness. As usual, John has huge problems with this because it would be like Al Capone himself testifying that what he says is true. In other words, there is no way to verify it. This "inner witness" of the Holy Spirit is not something that is really testable or provable. He compares this with the believability of an intelligent alien life form. He needs convincing, in other words. There is none available though; certainly none to his liking.

Remarkably, John makes statements like this as if he never experienced any of these things (the inner witness of the Holy Spirit, etc.)

when he was a "Christian." This leads one to conclude that John was likely not a true Christian in the first place.

There is nothing that could be found where John cites or indicates that he at one point experienced that aspect of Christianity. If it is in his book, this author did not see it. Due to this absence, it can only be reasonably assumed that John's experience as a Christian was devoid of these things. If devoid, then one cannot help but determine that quite possibly, John was never a Christian. Can John possibly blame anyone for arriving at that conclusion?

He then moves into a discussion of unanswered prayer, and here he does state that he knew what unanswered prayer was all about. Of course, because John has removed God from the picture, he does not really adequately deal with the aspect of God's *sovereignty* in prayer. On one occasion, he says he prayed that Elton John would become a Christian and would then begin producing Christian music. He prayed this way for years and finally gave up. Why? Is Elton John dead?

At this writing, he is still alive, which means that the prayer *could* be answered still. John has a timetable though. Not only does he want Elton John saved, but he wants him saved now, and he wants him to write Christian music. So God is not allowed to be God. He is a genie to fulfill peoples' wishes. Don't pray for someone's salvation simply because they need saving. Pray for their salvation so the person praying can get something out of it too! Remember kids, God has no real plan. He is merely waiting for His children to ask Him to do things.

It is likely that people also gave up on the individual who died next to Jesus. Yet, at the very last possible hour, he believed that Jesus was who He said He was and through that faith in Him, gained eternal life.

Evil is as Evil Does

John also attempts to deal with the problem of evil. It should be noted again here that John's entire book approaches Christianity from a philosophical frame of reference. In other words, philosophical arguments are either applied to Christianity or aspects of it, and Christianity (he believes) has been found wanting. It cannot be stated strongly enough though, that John is playing by his own rules, without the benefit of the supernatural.

According to the Bible, evil exists because Adam and Eve fell by disobeying God. This brought pain and death into this world, both physically and spiritually. John does not consider this and simply approaches the problem of evil from a "rational" standpoint. While this serves to bring evil into a greater focus, it does nothing to really answer the question of why evil exists in the long run. Apparently, this is John's "rock of atheism," because he believes it to be an impenetrable fortress that no one has succeeded in overcoming.

John takes the position of arguing against the theistic understanding of God. He lists moral evil, then natural evil (disasters, diseases, birth defects, etc.), and then the non-moral category of evil which includes accidents, and the like. From there, John discusses a number of potential solutions that have been espoused to explain the problem of evil: G. W. Leibniz, Augustinian, the Logical argument, Evidential argument, etc. These are all philosophical in nature and do nothing to provide *the* reason for evil.

Like most atheists and skeptics, John misses the point of evil to begin with and it is certainly clear that he would not like the answer. Before discussing the reason for evil though, let us deal with a world in which no god exists at all. In such a world, the problem of evil (which would likely still exist) cannot adequately be answered by the atheist either and certainly not by the evolutionist, except in general terms. In fact, one would think that the atheist or evolutionist would have the perfect answer for why evil exists, yet while they *do* have an answer, it is man-centered as usual.

In a world in which no god exists, evil would simply be a byproduct of evolution, which would then mean that it was not really evil at all, but simply a *state* in which things occur that people do not particularly like. Some individuals who have a proclivity toward evil apparently enjoy it, but most could do without it.

Why Evil?
The world according to the evolutionist is billions of years old. Man has evolved to such an extent that by this point, one could argue, moral evil should be a thing of the past. If man is progressing, then improvement is what should be seen. Is not man getting better? Oh wait, becoming civilized stopped much of the process in certain areas. It seems clear from history that there were pockets of time or periods where people were actually *more* morally good than they are now.

If man has truly evolved to the point where technology allows things to be created faster than ever before and science and medicine have reached the point of being on the cusp of eliminating some horrific diseases, why is it that the world continues to look as if it is going crazy; overrun with evil? Vestiges of the ancient evolutionary past?

Neither the atheist nor the evolutionist has an adequate response to the question of why evil exists. They have nothing. But they do not feel as though they *need* to offer a reason. Evil requires no answer. Religion (or more specifically, Christianity), must provide the answer to "Why does evil exist at all? If God is everything that Christianity teaches: all-knowing, all-powerful, loving, just, holy, etc., then why does evil exist? Surely God could have easily created a world in which evil did not exist at all, right?" Yes, and He did that. It was called the *Garden of Eden*.

God Created Everything Good
What if we were to say that the problem of evil exists because the greater the evil, the greater the contrast with God and His goodness?

What if God decided to create a universe and a planet containing people and animals that were originally good (for the sake of argument)? What if God also *allowed* evil to exist so that His purposes, and His purposes *only* would be accomplished (again, for the sake of argument)? And what if this same God chose specific individuals in this world for salvation while ignoring others? And what if God used the evil that existed in order that His purposes might *succeed*? Beyond this, what if God sees death completely differently than man sees death? What if God's ways are not man's ways? What if God does not have to answer to puny human beings who believe themselves to be god, yet are incapable of creating anything from nothing and completely unable to explain how life began on this planet?

Evil is *not* a formidable problem to God. He has total control over all evil. Consider Job and all that happened to him. God has adequately explained His position in that book alone.

What human being would come up with the story of Job in which God had the final word and that word silenced all opponents? No human being would be able to come up with that story, because any story written by a human being would end with the human being outshouting God and presenting God with questions that God would not be able to answer.

Unanswerable Questions?
The atheist and the skeptic believe that they have questions that are unanswerable by the Christian. The Bible says *"The fool says in his heart there is no god."* (Psalm 14:1)

Atheists are too quick to pat themselves on the back (another sign of arrogance). The truth is that they do not *like* the answers given by

Christians, and because they do not like them they *have decided* that the questions have not been adequately answered. They firmly *believe* that no god exists because of the existence of evil as well as other things. They believe the very fact of evil's existence trumps the existence of God. This is merely their interpretation of circumstantial evidence.

In the final analysis, their arguments are meaningless because they are not really arguing or debating with *God*. They are debating with themselves and other finite human beings. Because they receive the answer of silence from God, they erroneously believe that they have won because of that silence. This simply shows the foolishness of their thinking, since the answers have been provided in God's Word. His WORD. He spoke and responded…once. He is not required to respond every time an atheist gets an itch or has difficulty hearing.

John Loftus also delves into science to discuss the Creation account of how the world began. It is good to point out (again) that science has yet to definitively state how life began on this planet, but atheists and evolutionists alike seem not to be bothered by that, convinced the answer will come to the fore.

They also seem to delight in denouncing anything that has to do with I.D. (intelligent design). As a reminder, even though science has yet to provide conclusive, definitive answers for many important topics, their evergreen motto, "we're working on it," seems to be enough to satisfy even the most halfhearted atheist or skeptic.

It is worth repeating: if God created all that exists with the *appearance of age*, it would be impossible to disprove Creation. Impossible. In other words, there would be no way to prove that Creation did not occur as described in Genesis 1 and 2. Kids today…

Chapter 7

John Loftus refers to Jesus as a "Failed Doomsday Prophet."[41] This, he says, is due to the fact that what Jesus prophesied has simply not come to pass. In these areas of prophecy, John again attempts to exegete the text of Scripture, and it is unfortunate

---

[41] John W. Loftus, *Why I Became an Atheist,* (Amherst: Prometheus Books, 2008), 300

that his inability to do so due to his lack of understanding is so clearly evidenced as a result.

The author of this book has dealt with the biblical subject of prophecy extensively, some of which has been published in a previous work entitled *Interpreting the Bible Literally (Is Not as Confusing as It Sounds)*. More in this area will be published in the upcoming book, *When the Rightful Owner Returns*. There are also some wonderful resources that shed a great deal of light on this entire subject, none of which were used by John in his attempts to determine the actual meaning of the biblical passages he sites.

Setting aside for a moment the fact that John has chosen to label Jesus something that He most certainly is *not*, let it be known that there are very good reasons why the prophecies of Jesus have not *all* come to fruition. Some have and some have not occurred. The obvious question is *why have not all the events Jesus spoken of occurred?*

The Olivet Discourse is the main focus in the chapter of John's book dealing with prophecy. The Olivet Discourse is included in the gospels of Matthew, Mark and Luke. John's faulty labeling of Jesus stems from the passage where Jesus says, "*Truly I say to you, this generation will not pass away till all these things take place.*" John believes that since this was never fulfilled prophetically, then Jesus is not truly a prophet. Moreover, He is a false prophet, which means He is a liar.

While he is **correct** that it has *not been completely fulfilled*...yet, he is 100% **incorrect** about Jesus being a failed anything and when he stands before Him in judgment he is going to *so* wish that he had never made that comment and many others. That is tragic, but this author has prayed for John, that this sin will not be held against him since he obviously does not know what he is saying.

This and That
John's difficulty has to do with the use of the phrase "*this generation*"

in the passage quoted above, which he takes to mean the generation that was living at the time Jesus said those words. It should be clearly stated that John is by no means the first individual to bring this up. Moreover, regardless of how often this subject *is* brought up and responded to by Christian apologists, the reality is that people like John simply do not want to hear it. John and others believe that any attempt to explain this passage is simply a smoke screen thrown up by the Christian to direct attention away from an actual error in Scripture. This is not true by any stretch, but it does not matter to John.

To support his point of view, John also quotes people like Edward Adams (who?) and even Paul, whom he believes takes Jesus in the most "natural" way. John states *"The rest of the New Testament writers interpreted Jesus in (the) natural way."*[42] Here, John is busy again attempting to support that opinion, but is unable to accomplish it.

To his credit, John at least considers the context in this case, something he fails to do in a number of other attempts to interpret Scripture. Unfortunately, he does not consider *enough* of the context. It is really a shame that John did not reference all of the Olivet Discourse, or Daniel, Ezekiel, Revelation, Isaiah, Jeremiah, Joel, Thessalonians, Peter, and other epistles and books that deal with the End Times, which is the subject Christ is mainly (but not entirely) addressing here.

Regarding Paul, yes he constantly reminds his readers that the end of times is near, or more accurately, *imminent*. But John is confusing *imminent* with *soon*. The former means it *could* happen at any time now. The latter means it *will* happen at any time now. This is due solely to the fact that the Last Days (or End Times) actually began with the First Advent of Jesus Christ. For the orthodox Jew, there are

---

[42] John W. Loftus, *Why I Became an Atheist,* (Amherst: Prometheus Books, 2008), 301

only two ages; *this age* and *the age to come.* Imminent simply means that the event in question *could* happen at any moment, not that it *will* happen at any moment. Why should it matter what the orthodox Jew believes? Solely because the Bible was written ultimately by God, but through Jewish individuals. These Jewish individuals connected God with their culture and thought, using that culture and thought to express the truth of God's progressive revelation.

John – who states in his book that he was an expert apologist for the faith (my paraphrase) - should probably have spent at least *some* time reading and studying rabbinic literature. Had he done so, he would have understood that as this age moves ahead, it gets closer and closer to the second age, which is the age of the Messiah. In point of fact, the rabbinic literature sheds a great deal of light on Jewish culture and their thoughts and beliefs regarding the coming Messiah.

Since Jews penned the Bible, it makes sense to understand *their* vernacular, *their* culture, *their* history, *their* hopes, and *their* expectations. The Bible is a Jewish document. Most critics go wrong here in failing to recognize and appreciate this perspective.

Since Jesus is the Savior of Christians and believed by Christians to be the Messiah to the Jews, His First Coming has already occurred, and since He has already come once, His coming signaled the end of the first age was on its way. This is what the Jews believe about the "age," though of course they do not believe that Jesus was that Messiah.

The answer to John's confusion is a bit *complex.* As far as John is concerned, it will appear as though this Christian author is doing a slight of hand; creating a smoke screen. Nonetheless, the answer to the seeming dilemma is provided because John considers that he has found the proverbial final nail on the coffin lid with respect to Jesus' validity as prophet. It is because of that, the answer is set forth here.

Had John (and Edward Adams and others) taken the time to notice that the disciples asked *three* questions and wanted *three* signs of Jesus, their results might have been different (read: *more accurate*). Jesus does not answer the questions in order, nor are the three answers given in all three of the gospels in which the Olivet Discourse appears.

The Olivet Discourse is a long discourse. It covers a great deal of ground, most dealing with the final seven years this planet will experience. Part of what Jesus discusses here refers only to the event that occurred in A.D. 70, which we will get to in a bit. The remainder of the Olivet Discourse refers to the final aspect of this age that we are now living in.

In reading the text carefully, the student of the Bible will clearly see and understand this. John cannot see it because he has not read things carefully, nor has he allowed Scripture to interpret itself, nor has he utilized the culture or vernacular of the people who penned Scripture.

The Olivet Discourse is complex, as Shakespeare's *Hamlet* is complex. Neither are beyond comprehension however, and neither are able to be understood with merely a cursory reading, or scan. It takes some amount of time to sift through things. Though this author could be wrong, it appears as though John merely parroted what others have stated about this section of Scripture.

Not Enough Context
Starting off, John makes a very common mistake. Even though he states he is using the context, he fails to use the *entire* context. By the time we get to Matthew 24:29-34, with Jesus making the infamous *"this generation"* comment, Jesus has already described the event that will occur roughly 40 years later. He has also described in general terms (but with some specifics), the entire Tribulation and Great Tribulation, which is a total of seven years, ending this first age. Je-

sus has also announced the Temple's upcoming destruction (Matthew 24:2), as He and His disciples stood before the current Temple of their day, which took Herod roughly 50 years to build. By the way, it is accurate to state that Herod built the Temple, even though he did not do the physical labor of actually building it. He is credited with it, nonetheless because it was his idea and it was built during his rule. Please note that Jesus' reference to the Temple is in verse two of the same chapter.

The Reason for the Olivet Discourse

The Olivet Discourse is included in Scripture *"to answer the question: When and how would the Messianic Kingdom come into being?"*[43] Because Israel rejected Christ, Jesus could not set up His kingdom at that time. His physical kingdom would come to earth at a later time (thus, the Second Coming).

Christ introduces the Olivet Discourse with these words in Matthew 23:39: *"I tell you, you will not see me again, until you say, 'Blessed is he who comes in the name of the Lord.'"* Jesus is speaking *to* the nation of Israel here, not His disciples, since it was the nation's leaders that rejected Him.

To get a clear picture of everything Christ is teaching regarding the End Times, one *must* consider all three gospels where the Olivet Discourse appears. It will not work to simply look at one or two of the gospels thinking they say the same thing. No one gospel writer recorded everything Jesus said. Each individual gospel writer only recorded the information he felt was best suited to the theme of his particular gospel book.

The Three Questions

Three questions were asked of Jesus, along with three signs (when

---

[43] Arnold G. Fruchtenbaum, *Footsteps of the Messiah* (San Antonio: Ariel Ministries 2003), 621

the Matthew, Mark and Luke accounts are all taken into consideration together):

1. *"Tell us, when will these things be?"*
2. *"What will be the sign of your coming?"*
3. *"and of the close of the age?"*

The question the disciples ask in the Mark 13 passage is more specific in nature, *"what will be the sign when all these things are about to be accomplished?"* Based on what we know about how the rabbis looked at the 'ages' of the world (this age and the next age), the question being asked is really *"What is the sign that the very last part of this age has actually begun, that will ultimately lead into the Messianic Age when you (Jesus) will rule here on earth?"*

Interestingly enough, Jesus does not answer the questions in the order in which they were asked. He answers the third question first, the first question second and the second question third (this can only be determined by reading all three accounts side by side; feel free to verify this on your own).

Matthew and Mark record the answers for the second and third questions, but they ignore the first question altogether. Luke (good ol' Luke) is the one who actually records Jesus' response to the first question. If Luke to a large extent is ignored by the student of the Bible, then this question goes without an answer.

Most of what Jesus states in the Olivet Discourse is given chronologically, however *some* of it is out of order. Only a careful reading of the three texts will allow the reader to understand that this is the case.

What Are Not Signs

The disciples come to Jesus privately and ask him their questions. Jesus responds by answering their third question first (the sign of the end of the age; cf. verse 4), *then* deals with the sign of His Second

Coming. Jesus explains the entire sequence of time which leads up to the end of this age (the first age).

As He begins responding to them, Jesus provides some *general characteristics* of this age. Things like wars, earthquakes, false prophets, etc., will be part of this age. These things do *not* mean that the end has begun. False messiahs and local wars in various places throughout the world would characterize the *entire age* before the beginning of the end. This has certainly been the case and will continue to be the case until the beginning of the end starts.

Christ states (in Matthew 24:6), "*See that you are not alarmed, for this must take place, but the end is not yet.*" These two signs would *not* mean the end was beginning, so there was no need to worry.

The Third Question
Now that Jesus has introduced the things that would lead up to, but *not be* the sign that signals the end has begun, He next answers the *third* question that had been asked, by stating in verse seven, "*For nation will rise against nation, and kingdom against kingdom, and there will be famines and earthquakes in various places. All these are but the beginning of the birth pains.*"

Jesus has just told the disciples the sign that they should look for, which signals the beginning of the end. Now it is obvious that since this particular sign did *not* occur during their lives, and since Jesus is referring to the end of the age, then He was looking into the future.

The sign that should be looked for, is when *nation ris[es] against nation and kingdom against kingdom.* This (or is it *that*?) sign will signal the beginning of the end. The sign, coupled with *famines* and *earthquakes* in various places will signal the *beginning of birth pains.* Jesus relates the end to child birth. Just as birth pains, or contractions, tell the mother that the end (time of birth) is near, the sign that He has spoken of signals the end is near as well.

When a mother experiences contractions, she knows that while this is *not* the birth itself, it is a signal that the birth is drawing near. So Jesus is indicating that believers should look for this sign:

- Nation rising against nation, kingdom against kingdom;
- Coupled with earthquakes and famines.

When this sign occurs, it should be viewed as contractions prior to child birth.

In review then, we note that Jesus has first stated the things that will happen, which are <u>not</u> to be considered signs that will mark the beginning of the end. Then he tells the disciples what sign <u>will</u> signal the beginning of the end.

What is simply needed then is to find out what that particular sign means. At first glance, it means "when nations fight." If that is it, it is not much of a sign, is it? Nations have been fighting nearly since the dawn of time. If that *sign* means that, it is of no use at all.

Jewish Idiom

However, to understand this sign, one need go no further than the Jewish culture. In doing so, we find that this is first and foremost, a **Jewish idiom**. *"This expression is a Hebrew idiom for a world war. Jesus' statement here is that when a world war occurs, rather than merely a local war, that world war would signal that the end of the age had begun."*[44] This can be confirmed in the writings of the rabbis. *"The rabbis clearly taught that a worldwide conflict would signal the coming of the Messiah. Jesus corrected this idea slightly, for He said that when the world war occurs, while it does not signal the coming of the Messiah, it will signal that the end of the age as begun."*[45]

---

[44] Arnold G. Fruchtenbaum, *Footsteps of the Messiah* (San Antonio: Ariel Ministries 2003), 626
[45] Arnold G. Fruchtenbaum, *Footsteps of the Messiah* (San Antonio: Ariel Ministries 2003), 627

As people know (except apparently Richard Abanes; cf. *End-Times Visions*), World War I took place in 1914-1918. With the exception of two historians (both now deceased, whom Abanes cited), in effect all historians agree that this war was the first official *global conflict*. Abanes believes that the actual first world war was the *War of Spanish Succession*. However, unlike the War of Spanish Succession, there were over 100 countries involved in World War I, and the fighting during this war extended to every continent. World War II basically picked up where World War I left off.

World War I gave rise to the Zionist movement, and World War II was the catalyst that eventually led to the recreation of the Jewish state of Israel in 1948.

What about the famines and earthquakes? Did they occur during that time? Yes, they did. Abanes though, rejects this information because he does not see that there was an *increase* in earthquakes and famines during or shortly after World War I. Unfortunately for Abanes, an increase is not necessary. Jesus never mentioned that there would be an *increase* in famines and earthquakes. He simply said that there would be earthquakes and famines connected to the "nation shall rise against nation" sign.

Note what Abanes says: *"But once more, history reveals that proponents of the 'we're-in-the-last-of-the-last-days' mentality are mistaken. World War I was not even really the **first** world war. That, according to historians, was actually the War of Spanish Succession (1702-1713). This conflict involved France, Britain, Holland and Austria. Historians R.R. Palmer and Joel Colton note that this was the true first world war because 'it involved the overseas world together with the leading powers of Europe.' The legitimate second world war was the Seven Year's*

War (1756-1763). It involved all four continents and all of the major oceans."[46]

It is always fascinating to see that if people look long and hard enough, they will likely find someone who agrees with their view. So it was that Abanes was able to locate *two* historians that proved his point. One has to wonder how long and hard Abanes looked to find these two gentlemen, who essentially stand in opposition to virtually every other historian? These are the lengths that people will go to prove their point, even if it winds up not being proven in the end.

At any rate, we see that Jesus told His disciples that the one sign that would signal the beginning of the end was global conflict. *World War I was that sign* (in spite of Abanes' erroneous belief). Based on this fact alone, it then becomes impossible to understand the phrase "this generation" in the Olivet Discourse as referring to the generation that was alive while Jesus walked this earth. It is simply incompatible with that interpretation. But there is more.

Back to the Past (Jesus' Present)
Now that Jesus has answered the third question about the sign that would signal the *beginning of the end*, He refers again to His own time and highlights some of the events that the apostles would *personally endure*. This is recorded in Luke 21:12-20. The information in the Luke account unmistakably indicates the events *before* the sign which signals the beginning of the end. Christ says "*But before all this...*" (v. 12), showing that He has explained things *out of* chronological order.

After He describes the sign that would usher in the beginning of the end, He then goes *back* ("*But before all this...*") to fill in some blanks and add detail. People do this all the time in everyday conversation.

---

[46] Richard Abanes, *End Times-Visions* (New York: Four Walls Eight Windows 1998), 277

It is normal, and it is difficult to understand why some have a difficult time with that concept. Here is an example of how someone might explain their weekend plans to a friend:

"Well, let's see, Friday we're planning to take in my son's football game and after that we'll probably head on over to our favorite pizza place. On Saturday, we're heading up to the mountains to enjoy the mountain air and take in some fishing.

"Before that happens though, I've got to get the car out of the shop, so I'll need to pick the car up before the football game on Friday. This particular football game is the one everyone has been waiting for. It's huge! I guess the other team has some big secret weapon that they've been waiting to bring out, so we'll see what happens.

"Oh yeah, have to get our daughter over to her horseback riding lesson on Saturday before we head up to the mountains. It's going to be a busy weekend!"

So, if we were to organize all of that chronologically, it would look like this:

- Pick up car from shop (paragraph 2)
- Football game (paragraph 1a)
- Pizza (paragraph 1b)
- Daughter to her horseback lesson (paragraph 3)
- Mountain trip (paragraph 1c)

People don't always speak chronologically and we understand and accept that as the way conversations go. Why is this difficult for anyone to follow?

Jerusalem's Fall
In Luke 21:20-24, Jesus provides detailed information about Jerusalem's upcoming destruction. *"But when you see Jerusalem surrounded by armies, then know that its desolation has come near. Then let those*

who are in Judea flee to the mountains, and let those who are inside the city depart, and let not those who are out in the country enter it, for these are days of vengeance, to fulfill all that is written. Alas for women who are pregnant and for those who are nursing infants in those days! For there will be great distress upon the earth and wrath against this people. They will fall by the edge of the sword and be led captive among all nations, and Jerusalem will be trampled underfoot by the Gentiles, until the times of the Gentiles are fulfilled."

This entire paragraph refers to the events in A.D. 70. We know this because of what occurred then, some forty years after Jesus spoke those words.

Rome's armies *surrounded* Jerusalem and destroyed it and the Temple in A.D. 70. That was the sign that Jerusalem was about to be destroyed and when those in Jerusalem saw these armies, they should run to the hills! The sign that revealed the beginning of the end (*nation rising against nation...*) did *not* take place then. In fact, the destruction of Jerusalem in A.D. 70 has nothing directly to do with the end of the age. It was simply God's judgment on Israel for their rejection of their Messiah. Jesus refers to that event because of the discussion of the Temple started by the disciples.

An Example of the Space-Time Continuum
There are numerous places in Scripture where merely two verses shows the passing of thousands of years, yet does not indicate it in those verses. That information comes by comparing those verses to other portions of Scripture. This is referred to as the Law of Double Reference, by interpreters and scholars of Bible study.

For instance, if we look at Zechariah 9:9-10, we read these words, *"(9) Rejoice greatly, O daughter of Zion! Shout aloud, O daughter of Jerusalem! Behold, your king is coming to you; righteous and having salvation is he, humble and mounted on a donkey, on a colt, the foal of a donkey.*

(10) I will cut off the chariot from Ephraim and the war horse from Jerusalem; and the battle bow shall be cut off, and he shall speak peace to the nations; his rule shall be from sea to sea, and from the River to the ends of the earth."

These two verses run concurrently; one right after the other. However, it is clear from the text that verse nine refers to the Messiah entering Jerusalem at His first advent and verse ten refers to when this same Messiah actually rules, which is yet future. So far, there is over 2,000 years between the two verses, yet in the text, there is no indication that any span of time exists.

Back to Jerusalem's Fall
Notice the very last section of Luke 21:20-24. It says that *"Jerusalem will be trampled underfoot by the Gentiles, until the times of the Gentiles are fulfilled."* This is exactly what has occurred *since* the A.D. 70 sacking of Jerusalem; as part of God's judgment on the nation of Israel, He has allowed Gentiles to dominate and control Jerusalem. From A.D. 70 to this day, non-Jews have controlled and do control Old Jerusalem and the Temple Mount. God did this many times throughout the Old Testament with wayward Israel.

The reader is encouraged to research this information to discover not only what led up to the A.D. 70 destruction, but also to determine how *all Jewish believers* (Messianic Jews) were saved during that time before the final destruction of Jerusalem, due to a break in the fighting.

For a very brief time (circa A.D. 67-68), during the series of wars against Rome, Jerusalem was not surrounded by armies because the Roman armies had to go to fight another skirmish, temporarily leaving Jerusalem alone and unobserved.

The absence of the Roman armies allowed all Jewish believers in that city to escape unharmed, because they recalled the words of Jesus recorded for us here in Luke. These believers saw the *sign* (when Jerusalem is surrounded by armies) and knew that Jerusalem's destruction was near, so they hightailed it out of there.

During the final attack by Rome, Jerusalem was destroyed, and all totaled over one million Jews were killed, but *not one Jewish believer was killed,* since they had already left the city. This has been thoroughly researched as historical fact, by Dr. Arnold Fruchtenbaum. The reader of course, is encouraged to verify this on his own.

The Second Question – First Half of the Tribulation
Jesus has answered all but the second question. Here Jesus turns His attention to the Tribulation and the Great Tribulation itself, which are the final seven years of this age. The events of the first half of the Tribulation are highlighted in Matthew 24:9-14, and even though similar thoughts are conveyed in both the Mark and Luke accounts, Matthew deals with something else. It requires more research and careful attention to the verbiage used in order to correctly understand what is being stated. It is a small, but significant word: *then*.

Jesus says *"Then they will deliver you up to tribulation and put you to death, and you will be hated by all nations for my name's sake. And then many will fall away and betray one another and hate one another. And many false prophets will arise and lead many astray. And because lawlessness will be increased, the love of many will grow cold. But the one who endures to the end will be saved. And this gospel of the kingdom will be proclaimed throughout the whole world as a testimony to all nations, and then the end will come."* (Matthew 24:9-14) Here we see the following proclaimed by Christ:

- Unparalleled persecution
- Many false prophets
- Huge rise in sin and iniquity
- Jews surviving to the end will be saved
- Worldwide preaching of the gospel

Though small, but significant, the word *then* introduces a new thought, and the Greek word for it works just like it does in the English language. Jesus is now highlighting what is to come *after* the nation rising against nation and kingdom against kingdom sign which signals the beginning of the end.

"Mark and Luke described events that will happen to the Apostles before the sign of the first world war, while Matthew dealt with events of the first half of the Tribulation that would come after the sign of the first world war."[47]

If a person really takes the time to actually study these three passages in depth, he should arrive at the same conclusion as Dr. Fruchtenbaum, which is the only viable conclusion. People who say that Jesus prophesied something that did not occur are incorrect and their lack of study and research shows.

The Second Half of the Tribulation

There are eight things listed by Jesus that will occur during the second half of the Tribulation:

- Abomination of Desolation (first stage)
- Abomination of Desolation (second stage)
- Anti-Semitism will become fierce
- Israel will survive but many Jews will die
- A powerful false messiah will rise
- Many false signs, miracles and wonders to deceive the world
- Counterfeit sightings of the Messiah
- A hint as to the place where Jesus will return at His Second Coming

---

[47] Arnold G. Fruchtenbaum, *Footsteps of the Messiah* (San Antonio: Ariel Ministries 2003), 631

Jesus eventually speaks specifically of an event He calls the "Abomination of Desolation" (cf. verse 15), which refers directly back to the book of Daniel and an event of tremendous historical significance to the Jews, which took place in 168 B.C.

So horrendous was this event, Jews came to know it as the *Abomination that Desolates*. It was perpetrated by Antiochus Epiphanes who waltzed into the Jewish Temple one day, slaughtered a pig on the altar, sprinkled the blood around and set up a statue there of Zeus. Some historians even note that he put a mask of his own face over Zeus' face. So, Antiochus defiled the Temple with pig's blood, and set up a statue of a Greek god with his own face covering that statue's face.

Antiochus was of course, setting himself up as god in the Temple and demanding to be worshiped by the Jews. Christ refers to this event stating that when they (the Jews) see that event happen *again*, then they should run to the hills because the end (of the age) is near.

The destruction of the Temple and the repeat of the Abomination of Desolation event are *two different* events. It is historical fact that the Temple was destroyed in A.D. 70 by Romans, and literally not one stone was left on top of another. The Romans actually took each and every stone and melted the gold out of them. There was nothing left of the Temple except the foundation it had once stood on.

An Abomination!
However, the Abomination of Desolation did *not* occur during this event and by understanding other passages of Scripture, one can see that this Abomination event will take place in the *middle of the Tribulation* which occurs at the end of this age. So on one hand, Jesus is talking about the *near destruction* of the Temple, and the *far future* Abomination of Desolation that would occur in the "middle of the week" (the midpoint of the Tribulation; at 3 ½ years).

Christ then continues with His description of the Tribulation which will occur at the end of this age. A great many events take place that lead up to and incorporate the Tribulation.

It is after describing all of these events that Jesus says *"Immediately after the tribulation of those days the sun will be darkened, and the moon will not give its light, and the stars will fall from heaven, and the powers of the heavens will be shaken. Then will appear in heaven the sign of the Son of Man, and then all the tribes of the earth will mourn, and they will see the Son of Man coming on the clouds of heaven with power and great glory. And he will send out his angels with a loud trumpet call, and they will gather his elect from the four winds, from one end of heaven to the other.*

"From the fig tree learn its lesson: as soon as its branch becomes tender and puts out its leaves, you know that summer is near. So also, when you see all these things, you know that he is near, at the very gates. Truly, I say to you, this generation will not pass away until all these things take place. Heaven and earth will pass away, but my words will not pass away." (Matthew 24:29-34)

It should become clear (to those who can see) that Jesus has just described something horrendous happening throughout the earth which will last for a season of time (seven years). There are actually *two separate generations* that Jesus refers to in the Olivet Discourse; the one that would be alive and experience the destruction of the Temple in A.D. 70 and another generation which will experience everything that will occur during that time of the Abomination of Desolation at the *end of this age*. When Jesus makes the statement *"this generation will not pass away until all these things take place,"* He is referring to the *future* generation that will be alive when the repeat Abomination of Desolation occurs. The generation alive then will experience *"all these things."*

Stars Fell?

History has not recorded stars falling from heaven in great numbers, and the powers of the heavens being shaken. It has not recorded the sign of the Son of Man, which is His actual appearing in the heavens either. There has been no trumpet call that gets everyone's attention, nor has every eye seen the Son of Man coming on the clouds. Had these events happened, it would have been noted somewhere, and more importantly you would not be here reading this author's critique of John's book, or this information about the end of the age prior to Christ's return. Right after the Great Tribulation, all of these signs will take place.

Some theologians get around this by simply spiritualizing everything in this passage. Preterists claim that Jesus "returned" during the A.D. 70 attack on Rome, but He returned *spiritually*, not physically. Nothing in the text supports that viewpoint, though. That does not matter to the Preterist.

In fact, Jesus states *"then there will be great tribulation, such as has not been from the beginning of the world until now, no, and never will be. And if those days had not been cut short, no human being would be saved. But for the sake of the elect those days will be cut short. Then if anyone says to you, 'Look, here is the Christ!' or 'There he is!' do not believe it. For false christs and false prophets will arise and perform great signs and wonders, so as to lead astray, if possible, even the elect. See, I have told you beforehand. So, if they say to you, 'Look, he is in the wilderness,' do not go out. If they say, 'Look, he is in the inner rooms,' do not believe it. For as the lightning comes from the east and shines as far as the west, so will be the coming of the Son of Man. Wherever the corpse is, there the vultures will gather."* (Matthew 24:21-28)

You have to appreciate Christ's phrase *"so as to lead astray, if possible, even the elect."* The deception will be so great during that time, that if it was possible, even the elect would succumb to it. It is not possible though, that the elect will succumb. They will understand what is taking place and that understanding will keep them from falling under the spell of that deception. Atheism and skepticism alike are merely deceptions, used by the enemies of our souls to keep us from receiving the salvation that gains eternal life for us. The deception during this last seven year period will be so deceptive, that only the elect will be able to see that it is deception. All others will be thoroughly deceived.

Christ also specifically underscores the fact that this particular time of Tribulation will be so great, the world will not have experienced anything like it previously, nor will the world see it again. He is referring to something that takes place *globally* and it will be absolutely horrific in scale of evil. It will stem from a global, imperialistic government led by one individual.

In A.D. 70, when Rome attacked and destroyed Jerusalem and the Temple, that was *not* global, nor did the Abomination of Desolation occur. These things are still yet *future*, not having occurred yet. Since the original Abomination of Desolation actually occurred in Christ's *past*, as an actual physical (not spiritual) event, then there is no reason to suggest or believe that Christ was speaking figuratively here.

An Aside: Daniel
It is extremely easy to prove from the book of Daniel chapter nine, that Jesus is the coming Messiah. In fact, what is so fascinating about the Bible is how clear and precise it is on many things. From the book of Daniel, chapter nine, it can be calculated (based on the Jewish calendar) the length of time to the week, that the Messiah comes and is "cut off" (killed). The absolute unqualified *precision* of the Messianic promises alone go a long way in shoring up the integrity of the Bible. In fact, prophecy itself is one of the biggest proofs in determining the truth of Scripture.

Of course, it stands to reason that prophecy must be interpreted *correctly*. If people will take the time to do the research, they may be impressed with what they uncover.

No Brainer
Moving on, it is *after* Jesus finishes describing the literal hell on earth that will take place at the end of this age, that He uses the expression *"this generation."* The meaning should at this point be apparent.

Jesus is obviously referring to those who are alive *when those things He has just described* **happen**. This is evident because only a few of the things Jesus referred to have actually taken place so far in history, but two of the most significant events prior to His actual return (the Abomination of Desolation and the Tribulation/Great Tribulation itself), have not *yet* taken place.

Just in case anyone was wondering, Jesus has *not* returned yet. His Second Coming has not taken place. The text says, *"Then will appear in heaven the sign of the Son of Man, and then all the tribes of the earth will mourn, and they will see the Son of Man coming on the clouds of heaven with power and great glory."* (v. 30) Has the reader been able to identify such an event as the return of Christ *on the clouds*?

It should be clear that the intended meaning of the text here is referencing a literal, physical return of Christ in the heavens, where He will be seen by every individual on earth. How, since the earth is round and not flat? This author is not sure and the text does not elaborate. However, certainly a number of things could possibly help. Things like the Internet and Satellite TV, which only a few years ago did not exist, do now exist. While the Internet itself was created in the late forties, early fifties for military applications, it was not available for commercial use until 1988. By then, home computers were taken for granted and since that time, everything has happened at seeming light speed. The use of cell phones, Satellite TV and radio, the Internet - *everything* - has grown exponentially. What is happening in Iraq right now is broadcast live on the Internet. That every eye shall see Him is not farfetched, nor is it something that could not occur with today's technology.

If we look to Acts 1, we are told that the same way Jesus ascended to heaven (which was physical in nature), is the same way He will return *from* heaven *to* earth at His Second Coming. Since the text says *every eye will see Him*, then the choice is either to believe it will occur, or believe that it will not happen. However, believing or not does not make it so. God's plan and purposes make it so.

There is nothing in the text that warrants or demands an allegorical or spiritual interpretation. In fact, the amount of specific detail included in the text argues for an actual, or literal, *meaning* of the text.

Again, referring to John's attempts at exegesis in his book, he points to the Preterist belief that Jesus returned in A.D. 70, but even he says *"Preterists deny the obvious meaning of what Jesus was saying..."*[48] This author congratulates John on the fact that he was able to see through the Preterist misunderstanding of the text. Preterism for those who do not know, espouses that nearly all prophecy has been fulfilled with the exception of the last two chapters of Revelation.

Preterism is not Conservative

However, John mistakenly refers to Preterists as conservative. When it comes to Eschatology (study of Last Days), they are in no way conservative, but in fact are extremely liberal, allegorizing Scripture to suit their needs, specifically in the area of prophetic discourse, with no rhyme or reason for doing so.

---

[48] John W. Loftus, *Why I Became an Atheist,* (Amherst: Prometheus Books 2008), 302

Actual conservatives are those who understand Scripture from a literal standpoint, which is to say that conservatives understand the literal or actual **meaning** of Scripture (*for a thorough explanation of using the literal hermeneutic, see* Interpreting the Bible Literally...Is Not As Confusing As It Sounds, *by this author*).

It is obvious that in spite of his statements to the contrary, John is the one who is missing the plain sense and meaning of the Scripture he cites. He unfortunately does not *get it*, but *thinks* he does, which makes him not only wrong, but capable of being misled, and misleading many others as well. This is simply tragic because he bears the responsibility of leading others astray, as David bore the responsibility of leading his own son, Absalom astray. God would no sooner step in to stop John from making his mistakes, than He would have stepped in to keep David from making his mistakes. The only time God would do that is when it needs to be done to protect His own purposes, as in the case of Balaam and his donkey, another event in which John fails to see the point of this particular talking donkey.

The remainder of John's book deals with areas he considers to be problems with Scripture. These have all been adequately addressed by individuals with more insight and education than he showcases, so there is really no point in bringing them up here again.

The truth is that in the end, one cannot help wonder about the reality of John W. Loftus' version of Christianity. He states that he is a very passionate person and once he finds something that he believes in, he dedicates himself to that. He states that his conversion was very dramatic and that he "*burned with passion for the Lord.*"[49] That in and of itself though, is not the biblical definition for a conversion. John was raised Catholic, but after his conversion eventually became

---

[49] John W. Loftus, *Why I Became an Atheist,* (Amherst: Prometheus Books 2008), 19

associated with the Centrist Restoration Movement of the Churches of Christ.

This particular movement was begun by Thomas Campbell in 1807. Because of his specific views, he was eventually suspended from the Presbyterian Church, forming his own Christian Association of Washington. Eventually his son Alexander became part of this movement and it was formed into the Brush Run Church with the younger Campbell taking on the responsibility of preaching and debating around the country.

Adding to Salvation?

It was not until 1849 that the American Christian Missionary Society came into being with their motto, "*Where the Scriptures speak, we speak; where the Scriptures are silent, we are silent.*"[50] Unfortunately there are many *implications* and *inferences* in Scripture that while not obviously stated, mean something nonetheless, *when Scripture is allowed to interpret itself.* Eventually, Disciples of Christ and Churches of Christ were born with varying theological emphases throughout. Some use musical instruments, others forbid them, etc.

In general, these churches are considered to be conservative or even fundamental. Many though, consider these groups to be cultish because of what is considered to be heretical doctrinal positions held. Their motto alone is reason for a bit of concern.

Some, for instance, hold that without water baptism, there is no salvation. This is not taught in Scripture. The "Church of Christ" teaches that a sinner is forgiven of sin when he is baptized in water by a Campbellite elder. This is nowhere taught in Scripture (cf. Ephesians 2; Matthew 3:11; Luke 24:47; Acts 3:19; Acts 5:31; Acts 10:43; Acts

---

[50] http://www.georgiaencyclopedia.org/nge/Article.jsp?id=h-1580

20:21; Romans 1:16; Romans 4:5; et.al.). Obviously, this is a huge departure from Scripture.

This author would point to the thief on the cross who had no time to get down from the cross and be baptized in water, yet was told by Jesus that he would be with Him in paradise. Obviously, salvation depends upon faith in Christ's work alone, not water baptism, or any other work of man. Christ's substitutionary atonement is either all sufficient, or is not at all sufficient. Cults always add to Scripture.

Whether the Church of Christ is to be considered aberrant or not does not matter here. It is clear that John Loftus, while being passionate about Jesus, may have merely been passionate regarding his beliefs *about* Jesus. Was John a Christian who eventually walked away from Christ? Based on election, the answer is a firm 'no.' Arminians would say that it is possible (those who believe salvation can be gained or lost, but that view removes God's sovereignty).

What *is* clear is that John Loftus, at least at one point, *professed* to be a Christian. It is interesting to note that in an email to this author, John unhesitatingly pointed out that there is only one type of Christian: *professing*. He stated that no one can know that they are truly a Christian. He would actually argue that since there is no God, Christianity is worthless and no one can be a Christian, if using the biblical definition. That is not only an arrogant statement, but one that is solely based on his experience (or lack of it), and his particular set of current beliefs. There are many such statements of overconfidence in John's book.

In some ways, the author's heart goes out to John, though John would say he does not need or want that. He says he respects Christians, but he believes they are simply wrong and even deluded. To be sure, John likely feels very sorry for the Christian, but it is pity born of overconfidence and error. In any case, one does not respect someone while pitying them for their perceived error.

It would have been enjoyable to read a book that had been much better researched. So many things that John finds as contradictory or problematic are in actuality not problematic at all. His book falls flat in many places due to his lack of journalistic research and integrity.

Christianity is Hole-y

John's views are his own, but for him to suggest (as all atheists and skeptics do), that Christianity is so filled with holes that it is difficult to view it favorably, is simply wrong. John has not sufficiently done his homework and the sad part of it is the fact that his book was published in 2008. In that case, the information that the author of this book was able to locate and bring to bear on any number of alleged difficulties spoken of in John's book, would have been there when John was doing the research for his book. It is a shame that he either did not avail himself of that same information, or did not like the answers he found during his research. In either case, it likely would have brought no different result for John, whose eyes long ago became sealed shut to the possibility of Christianity holding any truth whatsoever.

The problem of the ex-Christian is not new, nor is a novelty. It is not something that is new to the year 2009. The ex-Christian was alive during Christ's life and since. While Jesus was certainly saddened to see people reject Him, He also understood that this was the way it was to be, based on the fact of election. Those earmarked for salvation will be saved. The remainder will not be saved. Since it is clear from Scripture that no one *deserves* to be saved at all, the fact that God saves anyone is testimony to His love and justice. Fortunately for us, human beings are not privy to who will be saved and who will be ignored. In that case, it is incumbent upon each and every individual to preach the gospel, by their lives and by their words. God will work to save those who have been called according to His purposes.

Ex-Christians will likely continue to grow in large numbers as this age winds down and segues into the next. The only proof that will satisfy the atheists or skeptics will be furnished *after* their lives here are over. Unfortunately, it will then be too late to change their minds about the nature of truth.

Like Christ, who did not chase down the Rich Young Ruler or other people who walked (or ran) away from Him, likewise we can do nothing except pray that God will open the eyes of those who remain firmly established in their blindness. We must be willing to talk to them, witness to them, and seek to help them understand the folly of their current "knowledge." Only God though, can open a blind person's eyes.

It is difficult not to fear for people like John Loftus who have arrived at a place firmly believing (remember, they cannot *know*) that they are in the correct place, based on their understanding of the evidence. If they are not correct, they will have lost everything.

Again, it needs to be stated that Christianity is the only system (religion, relationship, etc.) in which its Founder came to die in order that some would be given the gift of eternal life. No other religious system offers this, and certainly no other religious system has a founder who did what Jesus Christ has done.

The Masquerade Ball
The fact that there are people masquerading as Christians, who are in truth *not* Christians (but either wolves in sheep's clothing, or charlatans, or merely professing Christians, who believe themselves to be actually saved), has no effect at all on the truth of Christianity. None whatsoever. Christianity stands or falls on its own merit.

It is heartbreaking that John went through some of the experiences he went through. But one wonders why he was not able to think about Job from the Old Testament, or the words of our Lord who promised that since the world hated Him, it will hate His followers. He did not say the world *might* hate His followers. He said the world *would* hate His followers. Could He have been anymore clear?

It seems plain that John was a stranger to the entire process of what it truly means to be a Christian. He failed to understand why trials occur in this life, yet Peter and Paul and James and Jesus explain this clearly. Because we do not *like* trials is no reason to imply that God does not care. We sinned, not Him.

Too many people today believe that once they become Christians, God is required to make their lives pleasant and they should always come out on top. In fact, there are some very well known evangelists who have built their ministry around the concept that God wants you rich, or wants you to have your best life now, or some other unscriptural nonsense. A quick scan of *Foxe's Book of Martyrs* tells another story. People who go into Christianity without understanding this, or with unrealistic expectations, wind up as John found himself. They failed to *count the real cost of following Christ.* His life was no picnic, and neither were the lives of the apostles and many who came after them. The modern day Christian though is supposed to have a life that is worry free and always winning? Whatever…

Certainly at least some of the terrible things that happened to John were of his own doing and that is absolutely common to *all of us*. We then have no reason to blame God for not getting us out of those difficulties that we have gotten ourselves into.

Joseph was falsely accused by Potiphar's wife, who said he tried to rape her and had his cloak to "prove" it. Joseph ran from Potiphar's wife, was later caught, jailed and forgotten *by people*, but not by the Lord. Let us not forget how he actually got to be with Potiphar to begin with: his brothers sold him into slavery because they despised him, yet God had His own plans for Joseph.

Through all of his years of incarceration, God had not forgotten Joseph, whom He ultimately raised to be the second in command under Pharaoh. It was because of this position that he was able to save his entire family, from which the nation of Israel was born.

Reactionary

The most telling difference between John's demeanor toward, and ultimate rejection of God, and Joseph's consistent level of trust, is how each reacted when faced with trials. Where John reacts in frustration and anger toward God for not helping him (in spite of the fact that his own sin put him into his situation), Joseph came to understand that what his brothers and Potiphar's wife meant for evil, God meant for good.

Could God have saved Joseph and his family from the coming famine using a different method without leading Joseph down such a path? He could have, but for reasons known only to Him in the council of the Godhead in eternity past, He chose that path for Joseph. Since the potter determines what he will make from the clay, the clay has no right to condemn or question the potter for His decision of how the clay will be used. Joseph learned that lesson well. John did not. That is the difference.

Following Christ means doing exactly what He did; giving up your life in order that the Father can live His will in and through you. Ultimately, what is the Father concerned about? Whether or not you have two or three cars? Whether you have a larger house? Whether you are able to eat out five times a week? Whether or not you have $10,000 of disposable cash in your bank? None of these things. He will provide for you, but He is ultimately concerned about your *salvation*. This life is nothing. It is short; over before we know it. The next one lasts for eternity.

Jesus came, dedicated to fulfilling the Father's full will for His life. As God the Son, He willingly placed Himself in an inferior position temporarily, lived as man was *supposed* to live but had not. He became our example. We are to live as He lived, come what may. If we are going to call ourselves Christians, then we can do no less.

Being a Christian is an exchanged life: my will for God's will and my life for His life. What He wants to do in and through me is of His concern only and it is to that purpose the Christian daily submits.

The Christian life begins with a spiritual transaction. No ex-Christian can rightly state that they had this spiritual transaction.

Chapter 8

"The fool says in his heart there is no god" – Psalm 14:1

The phrase "There is no god" is often stated by the atheist or skeptic as if it was a fact that had long ago been proven. The Christian however, in stating just the opposite, would hear a response that usually goes something like this: "Prove it."

The reality of course, is that the existence of God cannot be proven. Likewise though, the non-existence of God cannot be proven either, so when asked by the theist for the atheist to prove that God does not exist, this statement is usually met with, "*You cannot prove a negative. The burden of proof is on the individual who states that God exists.*" This is patently false, yet for too long, it has been allowed that they are correct in their assertion that a negative cannot be proven. But there is a huge problem with that statement and line of thinking.

The atheist or skeptic does not conclude that God does not exist in a vacuum. In other words, they are NOT born into a world where the subject of God never comes up. God is discussed via radio, TV, newspaper, magazine articles and books. There are churches on every corner of every town in the United States (that is a deliberate exaggeration to make a point, not a lie). Traveling evangelists hold revival conferences and meetings. Weddings occur in churches, as do baptisms. Religion is part of the fabric of most societies and certainly part of the fabric of the United States. It is nearly impossible for an individual to be born into the world and never come in contact with something or someone who does not hold to some type of deity.

The atheist's argument would only hold true if an individual was born into a world where (for the sake of argument) he was the only person who existed there (maybe the parents died off shortly after he was born, and he himself was raised by wolves), or that neither the concept of God or discussion of Him existed.

Since this is obviously not the case, and since it is impossible to go through life without hearing of or reading of deity in some form or another, atheists, it is clear, come to be atheists not because they are born that way, but through a process of thinking. They view the world just like everyone else does, and they are affected and impacted by all the information that exists about God. They process all the information consciously or subconsciously, and arrive at what they consider to be a conclusion based on their *perception* of the evidence. Because of this, they *conclude* that God does not exist. In essence then, they have *proven to themselves* that God does not exist. In doing so, the argument that a negative cannot be proven is found to be absolutely false, and they are proof that it is false.

So the natural question then is what evidence does the atheist or skeptic have at his disposal which allows him to conclude that God does not exist? It certainly varies from individual to individual, so the list here provides some reasons why folks become atheist:

1. A major crisis
2. New information about Christianity (or religion)
3. Too many denominations
4. Too many religions
5. No sense of a loving, caring, Christian community
6. No evidence for the existence of any god or gods
7. Religious beliefs are the product of wishful thinking
8. *No infant has the cognitive skills to understand claims for the existence of gods
9. God is a conjecture
10. I clearly acknowledge my belief in the non-existence of a god is just that: a belief--nothing more, nothing less (from an honest atheist)
11. Evil exists in the world
12. Christians are hypocrites
13. Science overrules the need for God
14. Evolution overrules the need for God
15. Philosophy proves that God does not exist
16. Believing in God is irrational
17. Belief in God is irrelevant
18. Believing in God is nothing but a crutch; a coping mechanism

Atheists become atheists *because* of the resultant answers to these and other questions they or other atheists ask.

Number eight in our list has an asterisk beside it due to the particular statement made. The information was presented as fact; however, studies are increasingly showing that this is not true.

Science is on its way to proving the opposite of this statement as it concerns infants. Consider this: *"Scientists from several fields have shown that from the first weeks of life, babies are active learners. They are busy gathering and organizing knowledge about their world. These milestones highlight young children's progress in developing perceptual and thinking skills."*[51]

More information from the same source states: *"Newborns begin right away to use and integrate their senses to explore their world. Most infants can:*

- *See clearly within 13 inches*
- *Focus on and follow moving objects, including human faces*
- *See all colors and distinguish hue and brightness*
- *Distinguish the pitch and volume of sound*
- *Discriminate sweet, sour, bitter, and salty tastes*
- *Respond with facial expressions to strong stimuli (like odors)*
- *Prefer high contrast items and geometric shapes*
- *Begin to anticipate events (for example, sucking at the sight of a nipple)"*[52]

Yet another source provides additional information, and while the author of this book does not agree with their assumption regarding the evolutionary process, this statement has been included because of the fact that the connection with evolution was made: *"there is general agreement that infants are attracted to the physical and beha-*

---

[51] http://www.pbs.org/wholechild/abc/cognitive.html
[52] Ibid

vioural characteristics of people, and that such capacities are likely to be the product of evolutionary processes."[53]

One more source will suffice: *"Humans have many cognitive skills not possessed by their nearest primate relatives. The cultural intelligence hypothesis argues that this is mainly due to a species-specific set of social-cognitive skills, emerging early in ontogeny, for participating and exchanging knowledge in cultural groups. We tested this hypothesis by giving a comprehensive battery of cognitive tests to large numbers of two of humans' closest primate relatives, chimpanzees and orangutans, as well as to 2.5-year-old human children before literacy and schooling. Supporting the cultural intelligence hypothesis and contradicting the hypothesis that humans simply have more 'general intelligence,' we found that the children and chimpanzees had very similar cognitive skills for dealing with the physical world but that the children had more sophisticated cognitive skills than either of the ape species for dealing with the social world."* [54]

Aside from item number eight related to the cognitive skills residing in infants, all of the others in the list represent *observations* upon which a conclusion is based. In essence then, the atheist is willing to provide reasons why he believes that no God exists, because he *has* reasons he believes are powerful enough to have given him the necessary grounds to deny God's existence (any god). In doing so, he is unwittingly stating that *to him*, atheism has been *proven* to be true. Atheism then is the result of information gathered over a lifetime, or at some point within that lifetime, which may well be far short of the full spectrum of that individual's life.

If the remainder of the items in the numbered list is considered, it is obvious that all the reasons provided by atheists (for why they are

---

[53] http://www.massey.ac.nz/~alock/hbook/messer.htm
[54] http://www.sciencemag.org/cgi/content/abstract/317/5843/1360

atheists) are *subjective*. Someone may say, *"I went through a terrible time in my life, and there was no help at all from any god!"* Another individual might reason *"There is so much evil in the world – what the theist refers to as sin – that it is impossible for me to believe that there is a god at all, much less a supposedly loving God who cares about human beings."* Yet another person might state *"Any belief in a deity is simply irrational and irrelevant. There is no need for any god to exist, so why 'create' one for ourselves?"*

The theist will view the same violence in the world, the same sin, the same trials and troubles that people face (and will likely face many of his own), yet arrives at a completely different conclusion than the atheist.

The theist may see the same type of "hypocrite" in churches and understand the reason they are there as being far different from that of the atheist.

The theist may understand why there are so many different religions and religious denominations and see no difficulty with that and with the existence of the One, True God.

There are many, many reasons why people are atheists. When all is said and done, atheists have *become* atheists over time (however long it took to get there). This occurred because of the questions that they asked and the answers that were either given to them, or that they saw themselves.

In essence then, the process of becoming an atheist can and often is similar to becoming a theist. Christians are not born as infants. They must come to a point in their lives when they make a conscious decision about Jesus and about the Bible. It is over a period of time (however long that may be) that they ask questions, and are either given answers, or they see them. The process is really no different, though the result is miles apart.

The only feasible way to prove that God does not exist (and this would refer to *any* type of deity) is to do just that: prove it. But it cannot be proven. No one can prove that any type of god does not exist unless they were able to inspect every nook or cranny of the universe and find nothing. Even then though, what is to say that this God (if existing), was simply able to stay one step ahead of the search party and remain hidden? Moreover, what if a god does exist and this god is invisible; how would that god even be found?

Rather than insisting the theist needs to prove that any type of god exists, the onus is on the individual who states without equivocation that no god exists. It presupposes that everything, all avenues, have been exhausted and no evidence of God was found. Moreover, it also presupposes that no God will *ever* be found. It is presented as a statement of fact and *because* of that, it is open to scientific experimentation and reason to determine its validity.

Take two people who are viewing the beauty of a duck, for instance, or the intricacy of the butterfly. While each appreciates that beauty and intricacy, one might say *"How can people not accept evolution?"* while the other might say just as sincerely, *"How can people not accept the existence of God as Creator?"* Since evolution has not been proven beyond doubt and neither has God's existence, both of these statements reflect that individual's *belief* and world view. They are seeing the same thing, yet coming to very different conclusions about its origin and the source of that origin.

The atheist is really in the same boat as the theist (albeit at different ends of the boat), because in each case, no conclusive proof can be provided that will allow the gavel to sound with the judge ruling "Case closed!" Neither the theist, nor the atheist can provide proof of his position. It boils down to a reasoning within that stems from the questions each has asked, and the observations made up to that point in their lives.

Chapter 9

The Only Path of Truth

Ex-Christians firmly believe they *were* at one time in their lives, fully dedicated Christians, but now believe that God does not exist, making them atheists. This seems to be a common occurrence for many "Christians-Turned-Atheists": at one point supposedly committed Christian, but now devout atheist.

In direct opposition to the ex-Christian stands many of those who at some point in their lives, became (and remain) true Christians. Many of these true Christians admit as part of their testimony that there was a time in their lives when they *questioned* their Christianity. In other words, for many of us, Christianity has been something that we have *grown* into.

A Knowledge of
We recognize the fact that when we first became aware of God's plan of salvation, our knowledge of it may have been merely that: *knowledge.* While we thought at the time that knowledge may have led to a saving faith, it may actually not have done so.

Even though we prayed the "sinner's prayer" during or after a church service one morning or evening, the *reality* of what it meant to be a Christian did not dawn on us immediately. In fact, our inner lives did not necessarily change much right away, or even for some length of time.

Christianity was extremely mundane for us. In fact, Christianity was downright boring and unfulfilling. There were times when we found church completely fruitless and therefore unnecessary, had absolutely no interest in reading God's Word, or witnessing to the lost. What would we tell them? *"Do you want to become a Christian so that you can be bored and frustrated just like me?"*

For a good many of us who remain Christians today and have been for years, we would say that it has certainly been a very slow and growing change, based on a relationship with Christ that we were not sure even existed early on.

A Sliver of Awareness
In this author's own life, trials have been many and often difficult. Troubles in one area of life or another seemed to pound on the door

with growing ferocity. God at times seemed completely silent, as though He did not care. Where *was* He?

However, at a certain point in time (the timing of which was known only to God), a sliver of awareness began to peak through the darkness. It was a sliver that said "wait." What did *that* mean, and was there actually a choice in doing anything other than waiting?! Many of us waited, continuing life as we had known it, aware of being neither uplifted, nor yet completely alone.

Eventually, for reasons known only to God, that sliver widened into a crack, and then it became more of a small beam of light unmistakably penetrating the darkness that we existed within. From this author's current vantage point, he was enabled to see that God had in fact *never left* his side. He was always there, working and waiting...for *this author* to begin to see things *God's* way. Today, the waiting seems to be over.

Virtually overnight, what *had been* a complete and utter lack of desire to be involved in anything associated with God, became an earnest aspiration to *serve God*. Realizing that life had been lived with little regard for His will, it had finally and with suddenness, become exceedingly important to *grow up, leave the lesser things*, and begin viewing this life from *His perspective*.

In a short time, pursuit of a Masters in Biblical Studies went from goal to reality, a new church was located; one where the pastor consistently and faithfully preached God's Word, expositionally. A "chat" is not initiated from the pulpit, nor is it the comedy hour, so that people would merely be entertained, laugh, and say "Church was *fun* today!" It was hardcore biblical teaching; the kind that made you look inside yourself.

Pastor Verne preached (and continues to preach) God's Word, and it is that Word that is sharper than any two-edged sword. It can inflict pain in the heart of the listener as a means of chastisement. It can instill a sense of holy fear for a God who is infinitely more powerful than anything science will ever be able to create, grasp, or even imagine. The Word of God is also able to instill a strong and growing grasp of God's limitless love which He carries for His children.

For this author, God is worthy to be *loved*, worthy to be *served* and worthy to be *praised* above all others. He is mighty and there is *nothing* that will stand against Him, including atheists, ex-Christians, new age revolutionaries, or evolutionists.

In spite of the fact that many *real* and *true* Christians have experienced dark periods in their lives, we continue on with God, held to His side by His grace alone, refusing to give up because of circumstances. We know nothing is better, and we know we deserve far less than what He constantly provides.

The ex-Christian firmly denounces anyone who attempts to question the veracity of their Christianity. While these atheists unhesitatingly *know* what they were before they eventually became atheists or agnostics, the true Christians will admit that they have been through periods of not knowing; periods that they were unable to comprehend. Yet, they plodded onward, carried by God.

There are testimonies from many Christians who have had these difficult times in their Christian lives; some before and some even after becoming a Christian. One such man is a friend I have had the privilege of getting to know because his mother attends the church I now attend. With his permission, his testimony and real name are shared here. He is a Christian who knows that his life is nothing without Jesus Christ. He understands that if left to himself, he would have continued going from bad to worse. He understands where that road would have ended. God changed this man's life and of course, placed him squarely on the path of Truth found only in Jesus Christ (cf. John

14:6). God can do the same for the reader's life, because God is the God of redemption.

Here is Tom Hatter's testimony, who as you will see, cannot state unequivocally that he *was* a Christian after he prayed the "sinner's prayer." Unlike the growing number of ex-Christians, Tom had doubts about the reality of his conversion to Christianity because of what he saw in his own life afterwards. Here is Tom's testimony during an evening service at the church he has been a member of for some time:

"Good evening. My name is Tom Hatter. Before receiving Jesus Christ as my Lord and Savior, I lived a life of sin. I was living life my way. I did not have a real relationship with God and as a result, I made a real mess of things. My life was utter chaos and I left a huge path of destruction behind me.

"I was essentially dead in my sin. Had I remained on this path, my destination was an eternity in hell and eternal suffering.

"Through sincere prayer, I asked God to save me. I repented and confessed my sins to God the Father and asked His forgiveness of my sins. I know God has forgiven me because He promises this in the Holy Scriptures. The Bible says in I John 1:9, 'If we confess our sins, He is faithful and just to forgive us our sins and to cleanse us from all unrighteousness.'

"I understand and believe by faith, with all my heart, soul and mind that God the Father sent His only begotten Son, Jesus Christ to be crucified, buried, and resurrected for my sins, paying the ultimate price for me. He arose from the grave three days later, conquering death. He ascended into heaven to sit at the right hand of God the Father, and is my Advocate with the Father.

"I have committed myself to Jesus Christ and know He has saved me. I look forward with joyous anticipation to spending eternity in heaven with my gracious, loving, forgiving, and merciful God.

"I was raised in a Christian home attending several different Baptist Churches in the San Fernando Valley as a youth. In the early 1960s at the age of twelve, I attended a Billy Graham Crusade at the Los Angeles Coliseum.

"After hearing Reverend Graham's sermon, I responded to an altar call. I prayed the sinner's prayer and accepted Jesus Christ as my Lord and Savior.

"In retrospect, I am not convinced that a real conversion or regeneration occurred in my life. I didn't show much growth as a new Christian, but I continued to attend church regularly, seeking to grow in the faith.

"Unfortunately, as I moved from the influence of my parents, I fell from my relationship with God. It weakened until it became almost non-existent.

"I became a police officer at age twenty-one, serving twenty-eight and a half years on the Los Angeles Police Department. During this time I was exposed to the worst kinds of sin you can imagine as well as participating in much of it. Of course, I now know that any sin is too much sin.

"Sadly, I was still out of fellowship with God, weak in the faith and in rebellion. I was living a life of disobedience to God. Oh, I was a good cop and received accolades from men for my work, but God wasn't impressed, nor should He have been. As we know, 'works' do not merit salvation. I continued to seek the approval of men, while God took a back seat in my life.

"I sought God's help through prayer when in trouble, and He always answered, but it was not always the answer I wanted. God had a plan for my life, but I paid no attention to it.

"I suffered many trials over the years. Divorce and Family Court battles were a big part of my life. The damage to my family was immeasurable. My sin affected and visited everyone I had a relationship with, but most significantly on my parents and children. That is my biggest regret.

"Sadly, it wasn't until August of 2001, when my youngest brother committed suicide that God really got my attention. This was devastating for my family and me. Grace Community Church chaplain Phil Manly ministered to our family and officiated at my brother's funeral.

"My wife and I began attending Grace Community Church immediately. One month later, on September 11, 2001, the attacks on the World Trade Center occurred. I watched the deaths of all those people, and destruction of those buildings.

"I thought about the many police, fire and emergency medical personnel who rushed to that scene rendering aid, sacrificing their lives at that very moment. As a former law enforcement officer this sight was especially moving to me. I wondered how many were believers.

"My grown children called me on the phone that morning. We wept together as we watched the evil unfolding before our eyes. Five months later my beloved father, also a retired veteran of the Los Angeles Police Department, passed away.

"After twenty-eight years of police service, witnessing so much death and destruction, these events in my life opened my eyes to the consequences of sin, the inevitability of death and the realization of either eternity in heaven for the believer, or hell for unbelievers. I decided it was time to get my life right with God.

"Dr. John Street preached at a Wednesday night Grace Bridge service last year, on the subject 'Great Teachers of Life.' He taught from a passage in Ecclesiastes 7:1-4. It reads:

'A good name is better than precious ointment, and the day of death than the day of birth. It is better to go to the house of mourning than to go to the house of feasting, for this is the end of all mankind, and the living will lay it to heart. Sorrow is better than laughter, for by sadness of face the heart is made glad. The heart of the wise is in the house of mourning, but the heart of fools is in the house of mirth.'

"I did much mourning during the trials I just described. I am convinced that God taught me through the trials of death in my own family. I got the message. I have received, by faith, Jesus Christ as my Lord and Savior and know, by His grace, God has saved me and embraced me with His loving kindness and tender mercies. He has changed my life forever through these trials and life-changing events.

"I must take a moment to recognize the effort of my wonderful Christian mother in bringing me to the Lord. As a servant of God, she made sure I went to church as a child and learned about the gospel. To this day, she constantly shares the wonders of God and His saving grace.

"With God's help, she supported me through many trials and sorrows. I know God has a wonderful reward for her in heaven.

"I can't say exactly when my conversion occurred, but since regularly attending Grace Community Church, God has become a very real part of my life. I hunger and thirst after the Word of God like I never have before. The teaching of the Word by Pastor John MacArthur, and the ministerial staff, has been a real blessing for my wife and me. We feel very fortunate to be attending this wonderful church.

"And now, I have some unfinished business. In obedience to God's Word, I am here to be baptized."

When all is said and done, there seems to be a tremendous difference between the Christian and the ex-Christian. While ex-Christians will tell you of the many things they *did* while they believed themselves to be Christians, they will also tell you that at some point, they began to *feel* that something was not right with Christianity. Instead of looking deep inside themselves, they normally placed the full blame regarding their change in outlook squarely on the shoulders of someone or something else. While admitting any failures on their part, they also managed to minimize those same failures.

The true Christian on the other hand, understands that whatever happens in life happens because God allows or ordains it. God does that for two purposes: 1) so that the Christian will mature, and 2) so that He (God) will be glorified.

The ex-Christians have no such outlook on either Christianity, Christians or God. They default to themselves, focusing on their perspective, their desires, their problems, their work, their feelings, their whatever. They do not look at these things as opportunities for growth, but instead see them as problems that God needs to take care of...*for them.*

It is sad, but extremely easy to see that those who refer to themselves as ex-Christians were Christians in *name* only. There was no spiritual transaction. There was no relationship with Christ. There was no new birth. What they thought they had at one point existed in their heads only. Because it was merely head knowledge, never taking root in their hearts, the new birth leading to a relationship with Christ never occurred.

The new birth provides the reality of eternal life through the saving relationship with Jesus. The true Christian is saved not only from hell in the next life, but from *self* during this life. Each and every person daring to enter into relationship with God must at some point, give up the desire to serve *self.* Until that occurs, that person is merely thinking himself to be something he's not, based on outward appearances and inner head knowledge.

It is too bad though that these ex-Christians truly believe that they actually *were* Christians. Not only do they have the wrong impression of Christianity, but they also present that wrong impression to the world. They will be held accountable.

Ex-Christians do more harm to the Cross and name of Christ than any charlatan evangelist who is 'in it' for what can be gained from it. These folks did *not* possess salvation. They had a passion that drove them to do things, say things, even think things that *resembled* Christianity.

To Satan, these people are tools he uses, first to keep their own salvation at bay, and second, to keep others from Christ and His salvation. Satan provided something they *thought* was Christianity. He pulled the wool back from their eyes, allowing them to see it as a sham. Since what they had *was* a sham to begin with, letting them "see it" was merely part of the deception itself. Apparently it has some measure of "success" or the enemy of our faith would not continue to use it.

These ex-Christians are spiritually no different today than yesterday, when they thought themselves to be Christians. Unfortunately, they never had the required new birth that exchanges their unrighteousness for His righteousness. They were never Christians, having never entered into a relationship with Jesus Christ.

They *can* come to see the truth, if God will but open their eyes. Will you join me in praying for them? They will thank you when they see you in heaven.

Chapter 10

Now that we have spent a considerable amount of time dealing with skeptics, atheists and the like, turning our attention to other areas of the biblical theology seems like a good idea. Starting with this chapter, to the end of the book, each chapter deals specifically with one topic of importance related to the Bible and theology, but not necessarily related to "ex-Christians," atheists or skeptics.

The topic of this chapter takes a look at free will and election, beginning with our first parents, Adam and Eve.

The Garden of Eden was a perfect paradise created by God, specifically for Adam and also for Eve. It was in this garden that God set the man - Adam - and gave him the responsibility of taking care of it, along with the animals and plants.

Adam was placed as ruler over all he surveyed; all that is, except one tree, which stood in the garden with the others. It served as a constant living reminder of the one rule that God had given Adam: *Don't eat of that tree.* It makes no difference what fruit grew and lived on that tree. What mattered was that it was off limits to humanity. "Don't eat," said God. He meant it. " 'For in the day you eat of it,' said the Lord, 'you shall surely die'. " (Genesis 2:17, KJV) Lewis Sperry Chafer says "*It is therefore clear that in angelic realms, as in that of humanity, sin arises from the abuse of moral freedom.*"[55]

There is certainly much to learn about how God works and about the truth that is found within His Word. However, one would think that living in a paradise such as Eden, with its compliant animal kingdom, where it never rained but a mist watered everything, where the temperature was always perfect, and where there was no strife at all, would be enough for Adam.

Unfortunately, this proved not to be the case. The fruit from the one tree that was forbidden became the very thing that Adam wanted. It became a distraction and it really did not take much for the Tempter to push Eve over the edge into sin, and she in turn pushed Adam over. Now, technically, no one can really say that the devil made Adam and Eve do anything. He suggested it and even went so far as

---

[55] Lewis Sperry Chafer, Systematic Theology II, (Grand Rapids: Kregel Publications, 1993), 236

to call God a liar, but when all is said and done, what the Tempter used as the weapon of choice on our first parents, were *words*.

We are told that Eve was deceived. The wool was pulled over her eyes and it is doubtful that she really and completely understood what she was doing. It is apparent that she also either misunderstood Adam's instructions about the tree, or added her own (no one should touch the tree). Nonetheless, she is still culpable and fully guilty, as the record shows: *"The inner cravings of her own being responded to the temptation from without and she yielded to evil and thus repudiated God""*[56] Adam on the other hand, went into this situation with his eyes fully open. He knew what he was doing when he ate of that forbidden fruit. He knew that he was setting his will against God's. As Chafer points out, *"he was not deceived but sinned knowingly and willfully."*[57]

What Was Up With Adam?
One is forced to ask why Adam would do this. It literally boggles the mind to think that in an environment of perfection, Adam would be willing to give it all up by crossing the line that God had drawn in the sand. What would cause Adam to do this?

The really difficult thing is that according to Romans, all of us would have done the same thing. It obviously boils down to a lack of respect for God's boundaries, and a lack of reverence for Who God is and the authority that He possesses and wields.

The author of this book is a sinner, saved by grace alone, through faith in Christ's redemptive work on the cross. He possesses the sin nature. Though saved by God's grace and His alone, the sin nature abides within the author still. While free *not* to sin, by the indwelling

---

[56] Lewis Sperry Chafer, Systematic Theology II, (Grand Rapids: Kregel Publications, 1993), 211
[57] Ibid, 211

Presence of the Holy Spirit, in all likelihood, sin will continue from time to time throughout the remainder of life on earth. Unlike Adam, this author was not created and placed in a perfect environment, with a will that was directed *toward* God, instead of *away* from Him.

Complete, Yet Incomplete

Adam is a different story. Though not perfect, he was created complete and innocent. Being created like this does not mean that he was like God though. While Adam was created in God's image, it does not mean that he was created omniscient, or all powerful, nor does it mean that Adam had no ability to sin. Adam was created as a human being with a freedom to choose; a free will; the first of his kind, yet untested. He was complete in that he *lacked nothing*. He was placed in an environment which lacked nothing. But Adam probably began to feel as though he did not enjoy *total freedom*. He was not autonomous. He answered to Someone: the Creator.

The New Testament letter of James sheds some light on how the process leading up to sin works, when he states that *"each person is tempted when he is lured and enticed by his own desire. Then desire when it has conceived gives birth to sin, and sin when it is fully grown brings forth death."* (James 1:14-15)

James is saying sin *begins* with lust and when carried to its potential (the act itself), results in death, which means broken fellowship with God and a wearing down of things within the physical realm. To continue on that path of broken fellowship from this life into the next, means to earn and experience eternal separation from God.

Sin begins with lust. In essence then, we can say that even before Eve or Adam actually carried out the sin, they lusted for it and thus began their journey into sin. Chafer's comment here is noteworthy when he states regarding Adam, "*If he were lusting after forbidden knowledge and independence of God, he was fallen already.*"[58]

Lack of Experience

It seems that Adam did not possess the one thing that might have kept him from falling. That one thing was *experiential knowledge*. Arguably, there were two ways that Adam could have acquired this knowledge:

1. One way was to *actually sin and the resultant fall would bring about the experience of sinning*; one which would stay firmly rooted within the memory.
2. The other way would be to have God *provide that experiential knowledge* without actually having to sin to gain it.

It seems clear then that the second option is what *would* have occurred had both Adam and Eve stayed the course and remained true to God's spoken Word.

What Does *That* Mean?

When God told Adam that if he ate of the fruit of the tree of knowledge of good and evil he would die, one has to wonder whether or not Adam had the ability to fully process that? He would certainly have known that this was something to be avoided because God said he must. However for Adam, trying to understand the sorrow and pain of separation always associated with death (experientially), in a world where he had not yet experienced death or even pain, would have been difficult at best. It would be like trying to explain to someone who had no ability to feel physical sensation, what pain actually feels like and how it can hurt. Hurt? What does that mean? It is an unpleasant sensation? Okay, but what does "unpleasant" feel like?

---

[58] Lewis Sperry Chafer, Systematic Theology II, (Grand Rapids: Kregel Publications, 1993), 212

They might have head knowledge of what the word means, but have they experienced it? Or, what about people who are blind from birth? They see nothing outside of themselves, and they try picturing what a tree looks like or the colors of the sunset. These are beyond their ability to comprehend, as they exist in our world. Yet, they can in some sense know what we are talking about, though not experientially.

Adam likely had no real depth of understanding when it came to trying to figure out just exactly what death meant. He had not experienced pain in any form. He had not known what it was to have a headache, to stub his toe, to cut his hand, to have heart palpitations, to have shortness of breath or fatigue, or to experience any other health issue. One day, Adam was not there and the next day he was, as a full grown man without a history; without memories of a childhood. He had a relationship with God who *"walked in the cool of the garden"* (Genesis 3:8), and while Adam was not a caveman dragging his knuckles on the ground, he obviously needed to learn a great deal, since it is understood that Adam was not all knowing. Even in all of his learning, some of what he learned would only be head knowledge and not something he would have experienced.

H. L. Willmington says this of Adam, *"It has been estimated that the most brilliant genius uses but one tenth of one percent of his total potential brain ability. This means Adam was at least one thousand times superior to today's intellectuals. We are probably 95 percent blind to the total color scheme displayed by nature and 98 percent deaf to her many sound patterns. But Adam's five senses were tuned to absolute perfection. He may even have possessed E.S.P. He perfectly understood both himself and his environment. He apparently was able to communicate with animals (Gen. 3:1, 2) and perhaps all nature also!"*[59]

Yet, in spite of Adam's intellect and intelligence, it seems Adam did not possess at least an awareness of the experiential that might have kept him from moving *toward* sin through the attraction to the forbidden fruit, ultimately disobeying God's one law.

Non-Compliance

It should be stated clearly at this point that Adam's sole responsibility throughout this situation was to do one simple thing: *obey God*. Whether he understood the ramifications of failing to do so to any real extent was secondary. His job was to conform to God's expressed will and He failed to do so. Because of this, God was perfectly justified in pronouncing judgment on Adam and Eve (and the world) since Adam had been warned.

God is not culpable in any way, shape or form for what Adam did, or for any experiential knowledge that he (or Eve) may have lacked. Adam failed the test all on his own. "*It is certain, however, that, had the test been withstood, it would not have returned again. Its pressure was not to have remained as a constant experience until the first parents were broken down.*"[60]

What Is This Fear That You Speak Of?

While we understand perfectly what fear is all about and how it affects us emotionally, Adam had no sense of that. Why would he? There would be no reason because had he feared anything, it would have ruined an otherwise perfect environment. Certainly, Satan, the master deceiver, would have done everything to keep his malevolence under lock and key as he stood before our first parents.

---

[59] Dr. H. L. Willmington, Willmington's Guide to the Bible, (Carol Stream: Tyndale House, 1981), 21
[60] Lewis Sperry Chafer, Systematic Theology II, (Grand Rapids: Kregel Publications, 1993), 213

To show himself as he truly was and is would have been to give himself away, signaling something within Adam that he had not heretofore experienced. Why would Satan blow his cover? Better to keep things under wraps and hope to get away with it by coming across as the smoothest salesman who ever lived. In fact, that seems to be his favorite disguise. It worked in a perfect environment. Why would it not work in a corrupt and fallen one as ours is today? Adam knew no fear because he had not sinned. We fear because we do and because we are born in sin.

So Adam had no reason to fear, and the command of God to avoid eating of the fruit of that one tree seemed far away. The tree was probably something that Adam and Eve had discussed. It is obvious that Adam "forwarded the message" about not eating the fruit from "that tree" to Eve. Unfortunately, either Adam got the message wrong, or Eve misunderstood it. In either case, they could have easily spent time discussing the situation, and probably did.

"Why did God say we cannot eat of the fruit of that tree, Adam?" Eve might have asked.

"I have no clue," would be Adam's reply. "He just said we must avoid it."

"Well, then why did He put it here with the other trees if we cannot eat any fruit from it?" Eve would continue.

"I have no idea. I do not understand why and did not ask Him," Adam would respond.

Maybe their conversation continued with questions about why God would place a tree in their garden only to say they could not eat from it. It did not make sense to them. What was the purpose? In essence, they took their eyes off of the rule itself and began to consider the subject of that rule instead, determining all the reasons why they *should* be able to eat the fruit from it. Does there need to be a reason greater than just because God said *not to* that they ultimately chose to disobey?

To Obey, or Not to Obey
Unfortunately for Adam and Eve, the reason why God gave them that one rule to follow was so simple that it was painfully easy to miss. It did not require any depth of thought, or any deep contemplation. It did not require a genius to understand it. It was not the type of question that made a surplus of education obligatory. In fact, the reason was purposefully kept simple so that no excuse could be given if and when the command was transgressed, and in such a case, no excuse would stand.

There really was no other reason than the fact that God wanted them to use their moral freedom to *obey Him*. He wanted their allegiance to His command to be voluntary. It was a command that God gave and He rightfully expected it to be obeyed. He also knew that it would not be.

If we had quoted to Adam "*The fear of the LORD is the beginning of wisdom; all those who practice it have a good understanding. His praise endures forever!*" (Psalm 111:10) he would have looked at us as if we were speaking a language he did not understand.

"Fear the Lord? What are you talking about? Why should I fear the Lord?!" Adam had absolutely no reason to fear the Lord...yet. It is too bad that he seemed not to have that capacity, because it is that fear that would have likely kept him from making that fatal mistake. At the same time, fear would have ruined the perfect environment of Eden.

Unfortunately, fearing God did come to them, but as a result of their disobedience. Could they have obtained this awareness of what was evil without having to experience the sin and therefore learn experientially about fear? Of course they could have, and that is what they should have done. Was God wrong in not allowing Adam to experientially know what fear was and how it affected human beings emotionally? Not at all. The law should have been obeyed for no other reason than it was a law that God gave and He expected it to be obeyed. Whether Adam experienced fear or not is completely beside the point. As has been noted, the command should have been obeyed for no other reason than because God gave it.

Our parents fell. Their eyes were opened. Again, Dr. Willmington makes this point concerning Adam and Eve, *"Their eyes were opened and they did know good and evil, but not as God did!"*[61] Had Adam and Eve passed the test by *not* succumbing to the Tempter's snare, we can be certain that God would have opened their eyes to understand evil, *without having had to actually experience it.* "*Instead of recognizing the evil from the summit of the good, they now must recognize the good from the abyss of evil.*"[62]

Smarter Than His Years
In some ways, one has to feel a deep sadness for Adam; sadness stemming from the fact that he was unable to follow a simple rule and move closer to God because of it. While there is no doubt that Adam possessed great intellect, in many ways, he was a baby when it came to life's *experiences.*

He did not have anything that he could draw upon, except God's voice and while that should have been more than enough, it was not. Adam fell into sin and took the entire human race with him. God's righteous judgment fell not only on Adam but also on every living soul that came after him because as Romans 5:12 says *"Therefore, just as sin came into the world through one man, and death through sin, and so death spread to all men because all sinned..."*

---

[61] Dr. H. L. Willmington, Willmington's Guide to the Bible, (Carol Stream: Tyndale House, 1981), 6
[62] Ibid, 6

In a very real sense, Adam had it more difficult than we do. We know what sin is before we sin. We know how it makes us feel inside and we know the struggle that we go through when faced with the temptation to sin. We know the fear experienced after sinning and sometimes, when leaning on God, we know that fear *before* sinning as well. That fear can and has kept us from allowing the temptation to give birth to sin. Had each of us been in Adam's place, we would have done exactly the same as Adam did. God's justice and righteous act of judgment is beyond question (cf. Romans 5:12).

Who among Christians is not familiar with Psalms 111? A verse found there (or ones similar to it) can also be found in Proverbs 1:7; 9:10; 14:26-27; 15:33; and 16:6, to name just a few. Interestingly enough, there is a train of thought which believes that this word "fear" is better translated to mean "reverence." However, fearing the Lord means just that - *to fear Him*! We have every reason to fear offending Him, especially as Christians. Paul tells us "*For ye have not received the spirit of bondage again to fear; but ye have received the Spirit of adoption, whereby we cry, Abba, Father.*" (Romans 8:15) Yet, it is extremely important to understand that we must adopt a spirit of fear when it comes to dealing with sin and temptation, in order to keep from offending God, who hates all sin. As Christians, we are truly His children and heirs of righteousness, but even children should rightly fear the wrath of a parent whose rules have been broken.

Our stance should be like Joseph's who found it reprehensible to even consider doing something that was against God's just laws. Joseph's question should be one that we all ask when faced with every temptation: "*How then can I do this great wickedness and sin against God?*" (Genesis 39:9b)

Say What?
Holy fear is largely absent among Christians today. There is no real fear of God. We have reduced God to something that makes us feel good. We have devalued God's Word and in so doing, have elevated

ourselves to God's level. We erroneously believe that He accepts us for who we are and is "fine" with us as we are now.

Too many Christians in today's world see Him as a celestial Grandfather, who dotes on his grandchildren, ignoring their faults and foibles because of His great "love" for all of humanity. Is it any wonder that we are screaming towards Armageddon which will display God's moral wrath and judgment to the entire world? The world deserves what He righteously proclaims is coming.

Years ago, while taking a college level religious studies class, the professor stated that "sin is brokenness." Think about that. Does it not make you feel warm and gushy inside? It certainly sounds gentle and kind enough for those who are merely dabbling with the notion of God and religion in general. That definition is enough to make them feel okay about themselves. However, it does not take into account the way *God feels about sin*. It is reprehensible; an abomination to Him and there are too many Scripture texts that could be referenced here to prove the point.

If we consider the first act of sin, through which death and more sin entered the world, we see the exact opposite of fear. We also do not see a resultant *"kind and gentle brokenness"* either. What we *do* see instead is a firm defiance; a setting of our will against His and ultimately, against Him. This resulted not in brokenness, but in death; absolute, immediate and complete. Spiritual death *occurred* immediately and physical death *began* immediately.

It is a tragedy that our first parents did not opt simply to obey God and depart (literally "run") from evil. God is not mocked. Sin will run its course, God will judge and it will be permanently vanquished.

Chapter 11

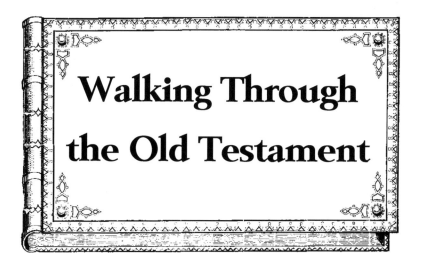

T he Old Testament, containing thirty-seven separate books, incorporates eleven of these as chronological: Genesis, Exodus, Numbers, Joshua, Judges, I and II Samuel, I and II Kings, Ezra and Nehemiah. These books together cover a period of roughly 3600 years.

The remaining books of the Old Testament fall into one of the following categories:

- Complementary books
- Wisdom books
- Prophetic books

Together, they make up the entire Old Testament of the English Bible. In order to appreciate the chronological history of the Hebrew nation (prior to even becoming the Hebrew nation) until the Intertestamental period, it is important to gain a solid understanding of each of these eleven chronological books; their themes, the periods they cover, and how they connect one to the other. Once these are understood, then the blanks can be filled in, so to speak, with the complementary, wisdom and prophetic books.

Genesis

Genesis unfolds the beginnings of everything, covering a period from 4004 to 1900 BC. Dr. Cone, president of Tyndale Theological Seminary, sees the overall theme of Genesis as being how *"God relates to man"*[63] Certainly this is the case as God goes through the process of Creation, with man as His crowning achievement, made on the 6th day. This aspect of God's Creation was so monumental because He literally breathed into man, and man became a *"living soul."*[64]

A good deal of ground is covered quickly from the first chapter of Genesis to the twelfth, but God seems intent on getting to his chosen man. *"Abram, therefore, marks a new beginning in history. He is the founder and father of what is called the Jewish Race; and the only man who was ever called 'the friend of God' (2 Chron. 20: 7; Isa. 61:8; Jas.*

---

[63] Christopher Cone, The Promises of God (Ft. Worth: Exegetica Publishing 2005), 16
[64] Genesis 2:7 (KJV)

2:23)."⁶⁵ When God first *"called (Abram) out of Ur, (He gave) him no promise (Acts 2:4). He later called him out of Haran, giving him rich promises (Gen. 12:1-5)."* ⁶⁶

God's covenant promised to make Abram's name (later Abraham) great by giving him a people that would be as the number of the sand, and giving those people an inheritance of land forever. Through Abraham, all the nations of the earth would be blessed (cf. Genesis 12:1-3; 15:3-21).

What is interesting is how God's chosen line continues from one individual to the next throughout the Old Testament, in spite of the many attempts to keep these very promises from being fulfilled. This is one of the biggest reasons the genealogies are so important in Scripture, because it allows us to verify those connections. Beginning with Abraham, we see that God's covenant continues through Isaac. Prior to the birth of Isaac, Abraham ran ahead of God and at the suggestion of his wife Sarah, slept with and wound up impregnating her handmaiden Hagar. Hagar gave birth to Ishmael who was not the seed of promise. Unfortunately, due to Abraham's lack of trust in God here, the nation of Israel has experienced nothing but problems because of the ancestors of Ishmael.

Isaac eventually marries and he begets two sons: Jacob and Esau. Esau was rejected by God even before his birth, with God choosing Jacob to be the one to continue with the Abrahamic covenant: *"Two nations are in your womb, and two peoples from within you shall be divided; the one shall be stronger than the other, the older shall serve the younger."* (Genesis 25:23)

---

[65] W. Graham Scroggie, The Unfolding Drama of Redemption (Grand Rapids: Kregel Publications 1994), 99
[66] Ibid, 100

It is from Jacob, whose name is eventually changed to Israel, that God brings forth twelve sons, who become the Patriarchs of the eventual nation of Israel. From these Patriarchs arise the twelve tribes of Israel, with Judah being chosen as the tribe of royalty from which the Messiah, Jesus Christ would ultimately come.

One of these Patriarchs is Joseph who, under God's divine election, was mistreated by his jealous brothers and sold into slavery. They did this to get rid of him, not realizing of course that they were fulfilling God's plan. Joseph who went from being a slave to becoming essentially the Prime Minister of Egypt, just under Pharaoh, was providentially placed in that position in order that the people who would become the nation of Israel would not disappear off the face of the earth during the terrible famine that was to come. To save his family, Joseph had his entire family, which included his brothers, father and relatives to move down to Egypt. All of this leads us to the next book in our chronology.

Exodus
Exodus takes place roughly between the time of 1525 to 1440 BC, and highlights the last stages of Israel's time in Egypt, followed by their exit. There is a break of approximately 400 years between the time of Genesis and the time of Exodus due solely to the fact that God's chosen people, Abraham's seed, had become captive in the land of Egypt. Joseph had long died and when a new Pharaoh arrived on the scene, according to the Scriptures, he was not aware of Joseph or how important Joseph had been. This Pharaoh turned the Israelites into slaves for needed labor projects in Egypt.

At the beginning of Exodus, a new character is introduced into the biblical landscape. Moses becomes God's appointed man in this hour of Israel's need to rescue them from their captivity in Egypt.

God, in His sovereignty leads His people out of the bondage of Egypt with the leadership of Moses, to the land that He swore (originally to

Abraham), that He would give them. They travel through the wilderness with God faithfully meeting their needs at every turn. Prior to entering the Promised Land for the first time, Moses meets with God on the top of Mt. Sinai and it is there that Moses is given the Ten Commandments. These commandments (along with 630+ additional laws, called Mitzvah) were part of a new covenant that God was making with Israel. This is all recorded for us in Exodus chapter twenty. God's reason for doing this is ultimately to show them that regardless of how hard they try, they will not be able to keep His commands. The natural question then is to ask why God would do this -- give people laws that He knows they cannot perfectly uphold. The answer is found in the life, death and resurrection of Jesus centuries later. In spite of the fact that God knew they could not keep the law, the people responded with wholehearted agreement by stating *"All the words which the LORD has said we will do."* (Exodus 24:3b NKJV)

In the narrative of the book of Exodus, God also introduces the concept of the Tabernacle to the Israelites as a testament to *"the fact of God's approach to man, and the way of man's approach to God. And as the Tabernacle is a type of Christ (John 1:14), we have reason to look for the counterparts of the type in His life and death."*[67]

Numbers

Next in our chronological line is the book of Numbers. Numbers begins with a census, which is a numbering of the people, and it ends with a census. In between these two censuses, two main events take place. First, since the Israelites have reached the edge of the land that God promised them, twelve spies are sent out into the Land of Canaan and all but two of the spies - Joshua and Caleb - return with a report that turns the Israelites' joy into fear. Joshua and Caleb are confident in the LORD, stating *"The land we passed through today is*

---

[67] W. Graham Scroggie, The Unfolding Drama of Redemption (Grand Rapids: Kregel Publications 1994), 171

an exceedingly good land. If the LORD delights in us, then He will bring us into this land and give it to us, a land which flows with milk and honey." (Numbers 14:7b-8, NKJV)

This report does not go over well and the two spies are outnumbered, with the crowd even turning on Moses and Aaron, stating *"Let us select a leader and return to Egypt."* (1 Samuel 13:10-11 NKJV) They are ready to kill Moses and Aaron, but God interrupts their plans and is ready to kill all of the people because of their threats against Moses and Aaron. God tells Moses that He will use him (Moses) to create a nation for Himself. Moses intercedes for the people and their lives are spared; however their punishment is twofold:

1. They are destined to wander in the wilderness for 40 years;
2. all those who rebelled eventually died in the wilderness.

As an aside here, it is certainly important to note that in this way, Moses was a "type" of Christ. Because of the sin of the people, God's righteous anger was aroused and had He killed every last one of the Israelites, He would have been justified. Moses, stepping in for the people, intercedes on their behalf, asking the Lord to bear with them and not do what His anger is seeking.

This is essentially how it is with those of us who have become Christians. At one point prior to the new birth, we were enemies of God. God had every right to destroy us, but because of His longsuffering, He did not. When we became Christians, Christ literally became our High Priest, interceding on our behalf when the enemy of our souls accuses us. Christ steps in and simply states that the blood He shed on Calvary's cross extends to that person who is being accused. God's wrath is set aside because of the perfect atoning work of Christ on the cross. Since He became sin for us (not that He *did* sin, but the Father looked at Him *as if He had sinned*), and Christians receive salvation from Him based on this substitutionary atonement, God's wrath is permanently set aside for each Christian. Those who do not now, nor ever trust in Christ's atonement remain under that wrathful sentence of eternal death.

When Moses stepped in the place of the people of Israel (by pleading with God on their behalf), he did what Christ did on the Christian's behalf.

The Israelites came full circle it seems. They started off with a census, mistrusted God, and because of that wandered for forty years in the wilderness. Another census is completed at the end of that wandering. This ensured that those who were with them when the first census was taken were now gone, having died during that forty year period. With those rebels gone, God is now ready to bring the remaining people into the Land of Promise.

Joshua

We now arrive at the book of Joshua and the conquest of Canaan can now begin. However, it is not long before Israel fails to obey all of God's dictates by not destroying everyone already in the Promised Land. Instead they allow some to stay, even making some slaves. This to their own detriment because they become idolatrous, just like the people they did not eradicate from the land.

People often think of the Old Testament as containing some of the most violent acts that seem supported or even demanded by God. The reality is that yes, there is plenty of violence in the Old Testament and there is a reason for it. By and large, the people in the Old Testament were very pagan in their beliefs. The chief problem of course was idolatry. Many of these various people groups often sacrificed their children to these idols; mainly the god Moloch. Moloch is described as *"the abomination of the children of Ammon"* in 1 Kings 11:7.

Moloch by Any Other Name

Moloch was eagerly worshipped by Canaanites, Phoenicians, and Ammonites. Israel joined the crowd and before long was sacrificing her own children, burning them alive during these pagan ceremonies. Because people like the Canaanites occupied areas of the land of Canaan and were involved in these reprehensible worship services, God had chosen to use the Israelites to destroy them and others who had been involved in this practice of child sacrifice. This practice had been in existence in that land centuries before God created the nation of Israel.

These sacrifices were done by literally having the child fall into a pit of fire from the outstretched arms of a statue of Moloch. The arms were made so that they were bent down toward the pit. The palm of Moloch's hand was open. The child would be placed into the open palm and then fall into the pit of fire, alive. Musicians were stationed in front of the fiery pit, between the crowd and the pit itself. While the children were falling into the pit, the musicians would play loudly to cover the screams of the children being sacrificed.

In essence then, one of the reasons that God chose to raise up a nation like Israel was so that they would acts as the vehicle for which God took vengeance on those nations involved in abhorrent acts such as child sacrifice.

Judges

Joshua gives way to the book of Judges as Joshua dies and the people are ruled by a series of judges who make decisions, keep the peace, and direct the affairs of the people. There is a continued cycle for Israel which consists of sinning against God, God using another nation to chastise them, Israel crying out for deliverance, and finally God bringing a deliverer for Israel. After this, Israel enjoys peace, happiness and prosperity for a time, until the entire cycle begins all over again.

This cycle continues for several hundred years until finally Israel decides that they want to be like their neighbor nations who have kings ruling over them. Samuel is the judge at this time and God tells Samuel that Israel has rejected Him because they want an earthly king to rule over them instead of Him.

I and II Samuel; I and II Kings
I and II Samuel and I and II Kings continue the Old Testament chronology in order, beginning with Samuel, who was the last judge prior to a monarchy being established in Israel.

Saul is appointed by God to be Israel's first king. Saul however, is eventually rejected by God because of what he does. He takes on the role of a priest and sacrifices a burnt offering and peace offerings to the LORD.

The narrative tells us what happens next, "*Now it happened, as soon as he had finished presenting the burnt offering, that Samuel came; and Saul went out to meet him, that he might greet him. And Samuel said, "What have you done?"* (I Samuel 13:12b)

Saul then recounts to Samuel how he had waited but that Samuel hadn't arrived, so he did what he thought he must do, stating that he "felt compelled, and offered a burnt offering."

Unfortunately for Saul, this was a huge mistake which cost him the kingdom. He was not a Levite and therefore not a priest, so God began to remove Saul's kingdom from him. Saul ruled for 40 years.

Another man is appointed to be the next king. David, son of Jesse eventually replaces Saul, and it is with David that God makes another covenant. God promises that the Eternal King - the Messiah - would come from his seed and that His throne would be established forever.

David's son Solomon eventually becomes king, replacing David after his 40 year reign. Solomon, who is seen as very righteous and upright, at first makes a few mistakes that cost him dearly. Among them, he marries more than one wife and unfortunately for Solomon, at least some of these women come from idolatrous backgrounds. Solomon gives in to them and has places built so that they can worship their gods. He himself becomes an idolater as well because of his wives.

It is after Solomon dies that the kingdom is divided between the north and the south. Not once is there a good king of the north and there are only a few good kings in the south. This division takes place in 931 BC. During this time, God brings prophets to warn and instruct Israel, but Israel continues in her unfaithfulness, eschewing God's chastisements.

Because of Israel's continued unfaithfulness, God declares that He is going to remove them from the Promised Land for 70 years, and He eliminates the Northern Kingdom in 721 BC and the Southern Kingdom in 586 BC.

Ezra
This leads us into the book of Ezra, which is primarily an historical record of Israel's return from exile to the southern area.

Nehemiah
From Ezra, we come to Nehemiah where the record of return is continued. Nehemiah leads in the effort to rebuild the wall around Jerusalem and it ends here with the people back in the land awaiting the promise of the Messiah. In fact they are looking for the one who would come just prior to the Messiah, making way for Him.

From this point, there is a 400 year silence before we encounter John the Baptist, who is Christ's forerunner, announcing the coming of the King, Jesus Christ. And the rest is the New Testament.

Chapter 12

There is an article on the Internet which professes among other things that a 15-year old girl named Margaret MacDonald is the real source of the doctrine of the Rapture. The article then associates Margaret's *"revelation"* with that of J. N. Darby's *promotion* of this same doctrine.

Of course, all who teach against the Rapture do so by pointing out that Darby promoted the idea in the late 1800s and because this was such a "new" teaching, it should be avoided like the plague.

What is the truth here, though? Is there any way to truly find out, or are we forced to agree with the idea that Margaret MacDonald is the source of this hoax?

Can History Help?
Let us look at history and see what we can find regarding the doctrine of the Rapture. For now, we will set aside Scripture, not because we do not find validity in it, but because we would simply come back to the same old, worn out arguments that keep people arguing over text and meaning.

We are all aware of Darby's belief regarding the doctrine of the Rapture. But is there really anyone prior to him (and of course, Margaret MacDonald) that espoused this same belief? If there is, then Margaret's incident is moot.

Fortunately for us, there are a number of folks who believed that the Rapture was set to occur prior to the Great Tribulation. We can show from history that the entire doctrine does not rest in the lap of a 15-year old girl.

In the year 1788, Rev. Morgan Edwards, a Baptist pastor in Philadelphia put forth the idea in his "Millennium, Last Days Novelties" book. He stated that he first *wrote* about it in the year 1742.

Was there anyone else who might have written about it even before Rev. Edwards did? Again, we are fortunate to have a number of people we can point to and it can be shown historically that they also espoused the doctrine of the Rapture.

A document referred to as the Pseudo-Ephrem document, dating back to the period A.D. 565 - 627 (or possibly even earlier) mentions the Rapture as a separate event:

"...For all the saints and elect of God are gathered, prior to the tribulation that is to come, and are taken to the Lord lest they see the confusion that is to overwhelm the world because of our sins."

So here we see just two documents in which the concept of the Rapture was taught; one roughly 100 years prior to Darby and the other roughly 1300 years prior. But, we are not done yet.

More Documentation

This view - the Rapture - was promoted by Bishop Victorinus of Petau (3rd Century), who saw the church departing before the plagues during the time of God's wrath.

Later, during the 15th - 16th centuries, Joseph Meade (1586-1638) wrote about the Rapture, 250 years before Darby.

It is also important to note that history shows the Church itself was Premillennial for the first three centuries. It was not until the Roman Catholic Church came into being (after the 3rd century A.D.) that the doctrine of the Rapture took a back seat. Many other important truths also took a back seat during this time, like salvation by grace alone, through faith.

The Catholic Church took the upper hand in squelching those doctrines with which it did not agree. They succeeded and it wasn't until Luther hammered his document to the Wittenberg Door that people really began to take note of just how far from Scripture the Roman Catholic Church had moved.

Unfortunately, the things that Luther, Zwingli, Calvin, and many others fought against continue to this day and show no signs of abating.

That aside, to be sure, the doctrine of the Rapture did *not* begin with a 15-year old girl, and then get carried to new heights by J. N. Darby! The reality is that the doctrine of the Rapture was a doctrine that was commonly held by the early church until the 3rd century, when the religious horizon changed dramatically and detrimentally.

Why Are There So Many Who Research So Little?
The author of the other article from the Internet who denounces the Rapture as having been made up states this: *"[J. N. Darby or MacDonald] dreamed this notion up around 1830. It always bothered me that for 1800 years every bible scholar and theologian somehow missed the truth of the Dispensational teaching. This included men such as Luther, Calvin, Knox, Tyndale and every other serious Bible student until it was unveiled in 1830."*

It would be wise at this juncture to remember Luther's utter disdain for the epistle of James because he felt James taught salvation by works plus faith. No one is correct on all things theological.

Apart from this, the proper response is to allow history to tell us *who* believed *what*, and *when*. The doctrine of the Rapture has been around for centuries, but was severely squelched until people began to read the Bible again for themselves. This took place right around the start of the 16th/17th centuries when Bible translations became available for the common person. Once the Bible got into the hands of the everyday individual, they could now read it for themselves. They no longer had to rely on some church official to tell them not only what the Bible said, but what it meant as well.

Enter the Roman Catholic Church
Up until the third century, the Church believed that the Rapture was going to occur. Shortly after this time period, the Church became closely aligned with the state and felt that it was wrong to allow the common person to read the Bible. Bibles were taken away from

people, locked up and only read to them during church services. They were then told what it meant by the priests.

So why did Luther, Calvin, and others seem to "miss" the Rapture and other aspects of theology that are routinely understood by those who call themselves Dispensationalists? The answer is quite simple really. Their calling was to shine the light on the heretical teaching that salvation came by grace *plus* works, through faith. This was the chief concern of the Reformers. They were convinced that the Roman Catholic Church had it wrong (and still does), so they demanded a reconsideration by church officials. Ultimately they left the church to form their own denominations because they could no longer agree that salvation was by grace and works, and it seemed that Catholicism was unwilling to change its position.

Salvation is More Important
This was the major tenet that they disagreed with concerning what the church taught. Salvation is not by grace and works, but by grace alone, through faith. This was the primary concern of the Reformers and for them, arguing about things like the Rapture made little sense.

While on one hand it is certainly wonderful that God used the Reformers to accomplish what they accomplished, on the other hand, it is clear that the Reformers changed little else within what would become their own denominations. All one has to do is look at these individual denominations to see that they all fell into the same trap that the Catholic Church did, by becoming closely aligned with the state and in effect, becoming state churches. The only thing that separated these new denominations from that of Catholicism was their understanding of the doctrine of salvation commonly referred to as Soteriology. They continued in the way of Catholicism in many ways, not least of which was the allegorical interpretation of Scripture when it came to prophetic events.

It is an Easy Out

The author's last question: *"Is the lure of an 'easy out' before the great tribulation befalls this world compelling because today's Christian is really severely shallow in their faith?"* has a great point. Are Christians shallow today? Yes, many Christians are absolutely and without doubt shallow. We are shallow, and our faith has very little root. Certainly there is an element within Christianity that would view the Rapture as an "escape clause" from experiencing any real trouble. That in and of itself is no reason for doubting the doctrine of the Rapture. It plays no part at all.

The prophecy of the Rapture, like all of prophecy, is given for any number of purposes, but undoubtedly the chief reason is to purify the believer (1 Peter 1:6-8, etc.). As a person dwells on and even meditates on being with the Lord, the idea is that their lives should then come to reflect His life. It should produce within the Christian the desire to be like Him in all aspects. A Christian is not much of a Christian who can live any way he wants to live, joining in with the world here or there, while going to church on Sunday. That Christian, far from feeling safe and secure about the Rapture should rather find his insides in knots knowing that he will face his Savior and that he will be judged according to his works; not for his salvation, but for how he lived.

If I am wrong about the Rapture, and I have misinterpreted Scripture so that I will actually go through a period of the greatest tribulation that the world has ever seen, so be it. If God chooses to send me to the mission field where I will be savagely attacked and killed for my faith, so be it. If the remainder of my life is one in which God's purposes are best met by placing me in a situation that is too horrible to imagine, so be it. Regardless of all of it, one thing is clear. When I do die, I will see my Savior and whether I am taken by Rapture or by natural death makes absolutely no difference. I pray that He will be glorified in and through my life.

The belief in and acceptance of the Rapture, far from causing this author to feel as though he is "escaping" something, actually causes him to bow the knee in humble adoration to God for His purposes, His will and His life. No one has any idea what tomorrow holds. This author could breathe his last today (as could the reader). It does not matter; but the idea that somehow believing in the Rapture creates weak Christians is patently incorrect.

Weak Christians: A Dime a Dozen
What creates weak Christians is their refusal to submit to Him and His authority. This is the cause of problems for all Christians who wind up doubting the Word, living a life that calls their own commitment to Him to fall into in question, and essentially dragging His precious Name through the mud.

Far from the Rapture weakening a commitment to Him, this author has found a greater desire to serve Him in what may well be a shorter period of time in which to do so.

The Rapture's origins are *not extra-biblical* and are certainly not found in the mind of a 15-year old girl. The Rapture's origins are biblical, espoused by the Apostle Paul himself. Jesus alludes to this event as well.

Salvation Promotes Licentious Living, Right?
The idea that the Rapture is a bad doctrine simply because it could cause Christians to take their Christianity for granted is like saying that salvation by grace through faith should also be rejected because it can promote licentious living (when viewed wrongly).

It actually does *not* promote that type of living. If understood for what it truly is, salvation *should* promote a greater desire to serve and love Him as never before. If it does not accomplish this, it is most definitely not the fault of the doctrine itself, but of the individual who fails to truly understand it to begin with.

Chapter 13

In his epistles to the Thessalonians, the apostle Paul addresses a number of important topics, from how to deal with disorderly, lazy and disobedient church members, to concerns about whether or not the Rapture had already occurred, to his reflections on the Day of the Lord.

Due to the rise of Preterism (the belief that nearly all prophetic Scripture has already been fulfilled, including that of Revelation), the visible church of today is falling headlong into a confusing and often heretical view of the End Times. More and more people are saying things like "Where is the promise of His coming?" (or the equivalent), and because of this it is of the utmost importance that Christians learn and hold to a proper understanding of the events associated with the Last Days.

While there have always been naysayers regarding God's work in this world, it seems that there is a good deal of uncertainty related to the events of the Second Coming of the Messiah, Jesus Christ.

A Foreign Language
Studying the Bible is very much like studying another language. We cannot simply start reading it and come to conclusions. The unfortunate part though, is that this is what many people do, and their resultant aberrant doctrine speaks for itself. Unfortunately, people really do not want to hear that. They would prefer instead to think of the Bible as a magical book; a book that once opened will release to readers the secrets of the universe and offer them the power of perception that no other book provides. Of course the reality of the situation is that the Bible certainly is God's Word; there is no denying or doubting that. Yet at the same time, He has chosen to write to us using *human beings* for the task, and in doing so offers us His thoughts about Himself, His plans, and things yet future, in a way that we can understand from our human point of view.

The Bible is God's Word to man and because of that, God expects us to understand it with the help and guidance of the Holy Spirit, who teaches us to rightly divide the Word, understanding it as God intended it to be understood.

Consistency Takes Work
Remarkably, understanding the Bible is often accomplished by the

rather unremarkable process of spending time studying the *culture*, *history*, and *language* of those who wrote it hundreds and hundreds of years ago. It is a process which must be marked by consistency throughout. In order to accomplish this, it is imperative that certain things be undertaken and lined up accordingly.

Language has changed so much over the span of time that it is ridiculous to think that we can approach any work of antiquity - much less the Bible - without really completing in-depth studies of the languages, culture, and history involved. In fact, it is absurd to think that we can lay claim to comprehending God's Word *without* using this approach, yet this is exactly what many people do today, if they even bother to open the Bible at all.

The problem then, of understanding what the Bible teaches about the End Times becomes great, simply because people do not want to go to the effort of untangling the idioms, figures of speech, metaphors and all the rest that are needed in order to understand His Word. People all too quickly minimize the importance of using a consistent hermeneutic.

What Does Paul Say?
Since Paul has written the lion's share of the New Testament under the careful guidance of the Holy Spirit, and since he is the one who discusses the End Times most often (with the notable exception of Revelation, written down by John), it is reasonable to conclude that our Lord chose Paul to reveal this information to His Bride through the Holy Writ. This he has done and ably so, yet in spite of this fact, confusion remains. Can we with confidence come to understand what Paul is talking about in his epistles to the Thessalonian church? What is the Day of the Lord? What is the Rapture? Is this event even *mentioned* in Scripture? Is the Rapture just another name for the Second Coming? Is the Rapture *confused* with the Second Coming? Is the Rapture man's invention? Can we show from Scripture that the Rapture is a real event and that it is separate from the Second Advent of Chr-

ist when He returns in power, authority, and as King and Judge to rule over the world? The answer is in the affirmative. Just as the archaeologist takes the time to carefully brush away the sand or dirt which encases a treasure of antiquity, so too does the Biblicist take the time to dig through the layers of God's Word to uncover the treasure of His truth. It takes a willingness to learn what might be underneath the surface of the words that Paul used. In the end, we *can* know the difference.

Does Paul Speak with a Forked Tongue?

Paul speaks plainly in his writing. He is able to be understood. The difficulty though, is when people *refuse* to seek his meaning, preferring instead to place *their* understanding on top of his words, which is called eisegesis.

If we consider just the passages in I and II Thessalonians related to the Rapture, it is clearly possible to obtain an unambiguous meaning that the Rapture is a real event and that it is separate from the Second Coming. This chapter will consider a number of passages in order, from the very beginning of I Thessalonians 1:10, which states, *"and to wait for his Son from heaven, whom he raised from the dead, Jesus who delivers us from the wrath to come."* From that passage alone it is possible to glean a number of things.

First, the Church is waiting for Christ to deliver her. Deliver her from what? *The wrath to come.* Just exactly what is this wrath to come that Paul speaks of here? Determining the meaning of that phrase will allow us to establish whether or not Paul is referring to the Rapture here or something else entirely.

God's Wrath

Generally speaking, God's wrath is always seen as judgment and His children are never to experience God's wrath at any time (cf. I Thessalonians 5:9), because Christ has already done so on our behalf.

Difficulties, hardships, tribulations, persecutions, etc., are all situations that we can expect to experience in this life, and we know that these occur for our growth in Christ; ultimately for our perfecting and certainly for His glory. But Paul seems to be talking about a specific wrath because he used the definite article "the" in front of the word "wrath."

Dr. Arnold Fruchtenbaum brings out an interesting point regarding the wrath to come that Paul mentions by stating *"The wrath of God here is future, and hence, cannot refer to the general wrath of God against sin which is a present reality. This wrath is future."*[68] Dr. Fruchtenbaum argues against the idea that this particular wrath that Paul is speaking of is either hell or the Lake of Fire since the Christian is *already* saved from both of those things. Because of that, there is no fear of them.

Consequently, this particular wrath that Paul speaks of can only refer to that period of seven years that is yet future; a period of time referred to as the Great Tribulation (though actually it is more correct to refer to the first three and a half years as the Tribulation, with the last three and a half years being the Great Tribulation). The Church will not be going through this, and it is for this reason that Christians wait patiently for our Savior to deliver us from that particular wrath.

A second passage in I Thessalonians is a very well known passage. In it, Paul outlines the reasons why those believers who are still alive do not have to fear *for* those believers who have already died, as if they have somehow missed the Rapture. This is what the believers at Thessalonica were concerned about. Paul states, *"But we do not want you to be uninformed, brothers, about those who are asleep, that you may not grieve as others do who have no hope. For since we believe*

---

[68] Arnold G. Fruchtenbaum, Footsteps of the Messiah, (San Antonio: Ariel Press, 1982)

that Jesus died and rose again, even so, through Jesus, God will bring with him those who have fallen asleep.

"For this we declare to you by a word from the Lord, that we who are alive, who are left until the coming of the Lord, will not precede those who have fallen asleep. For the Lord himself will descend from heaven with a cry of command, with the voice of an archangel, and with the sound of the trumpet of God. And the dead in Christ will rise first. Then we who are alive, who are left, will be caught up together with them in the clouds to meet the Lord in the air, and so we will always be with the Lord. Therefore encourage one another with these words."

Here Paul is without equivocation stating the facts of the situation that all Christians look forward to, or should. The overall concept here is that the Lord will descend from His place in heaven, and with a loud voice and the sound of a trumpet, will call his Bride from all four corners of the earth, those who have died first and then those who are alive. We will meet the Lord in the air and as Paul states, will be with Him forever.

Paul preempts any attempts to negate his words by introducing them with the phrase *"we declare to you by a word from the Lord."* Clearly, Paul is crediting Christ with this revelation. It is not something Paul made up. He heard it from the Lord directly (and not through any intermediary like another apostle), and is relaying the message to the Thessalonians.

But can this also refer to the Second Coming and not really a separate Rapture? Not unless the text is somehow *allegorized*, and this certainly seems to be the preferred method of interpretation these days. Even then, it is very difficult to assign this event to the Second Coming, when Christ returns at the *end* of the Tribulation period.

Mixing the Rapture with the Second Coming
Without doubt, Paul is talking about an event that is *not* the Second

Coming. How can we know this with absolute certainty? We can know based on a number of factors which are brought out in the text here and elsewhere.

When the Lord returns to this earth to set up His kingdom and judge the nations, His Bride is already with Him. Beyond this, if we compare a number of passages that are equally clear about the fact that they are referencing the Second Coming, it becomes extremely easy to see the differences between these two events.

Once that is seen, it is impossible to say that these two events are one in the same event. In fact, we will compare the descriptions of these two events shortly to highlight the differences. At that point, it should be clearly seen that the differences between these two events are certainly not manmade, but biblically-based.

For now, let us compare the I Thessalonians 4 passage with Christ's own words from another section of Scripture; Matthew 24. Here Christ states, *"For as the lightning comes from the east and shines as far as the west, so will be the coming of the Son of Man. Wherever the corpse is, there the vultures will gather. Immediately after the tribulation of those days the sun will be darkened, and the moon will not give its light, and the stars will fall from heaven, and the powers of the heavens will be shaken. Then will appear in heaven the sign of the Son of Man, and then all the tribes of the earth will mourn, and they will see the Son of Man coming on the clouds of heaven with power and great glory. And he will send out his angels with a loud trumpet call, and they will gather his elect from the four winds, from one end of heaven to the other."*

Considering just these two passages, frankly it is difficult to understand how anyone could look at them as if they were the same event. The differences are remarkable. If we compare and contrast them, they will look like this:

1 Thessalonians 4:13-18:

- the Lord Himself will come down from heaven
- with a loud command
- with the voice of an archangel
- with the trumpet call of God
- dead will rise first
- those who are alive will follow
- all caught up together
- will meet the Lord in the clouds
- will be with the Lord forever

Matthew 24:27-31:

- all eyes will see Him
- sun will be darkened
- moon will not give its light
- stars will fall from the sky
- heavenly bodies will be shaken
- sign of the Son of Man will appear in the sky
- He will arrive on the clouds in the sky
- with power and great glory
- He will send His angels with a loud trumpet
- angels will gather His elect
- from the four winds
- from one end of heaven to the other

Even a cursory glance will show that a number of differences stand out. In the Thessalonian passage, Christ meets His Bride *in the* clouds, whereas in the Matthew passage, Christ returns to the earth *on the clouds*. It is clear from the Thessalonians passage that Christians will meet the Lord in the clouds, but in the Matthew passage, no such meeting takes place. While the elect are being gathered in the Matthew passage, there is no indication that the elect will meet the Lord in the air, or the clouds. Note also that in the Matthew passage a sign will be seen in the heavens: that of Him returning to earth in power and great glory.

There is *no sign* at all given in the Thessalonian passage. While we read of a trumpet sounding in both passages, it is apparently not the same type of trumpet sound. In the Thessalonian passage, Paul distinctly refers to it as a *trumpet call of God*; a call intended to translate or Rapture the Bride from the grave and the earth. In the Matthew passage we read of a loud trumpet, which apparently is sounded solely to signal His return in power, glory, judgment and authority.

Moreover, Christ refers to the fact of a "tribulation" when He states *"Immediately after the tribulation of those days..."* What days? The days, or time period, of the Great Tribulation is in view here. He is pointing out by contrast that, compared to the problems and trouble of the Great Tribulation, His coming will catch the world unaware and everyone will see Him.

Signs in the Heavens

The most interesting aspect of the above referenced passages is the fact that the Matthew passage speaks of *major things* occurring in the heavens *before* the appearance of Jesus in the sky, arriving on the clouds in great power and glory.

The sun stops shining and because of that, the light that is normally reflected off the surface of the moon is no longer reflected. Stars fall from the heavens and other catastrophic events take place, along with some type of heavenly earthquake. This is all done as a means of announcing what is about to occur: the Lord's *Second Coming*. None of this is evidenced in the Thessalonians passage, which means that the event that Paul is referring to is pretty much a secret that will not be heralded throughout the world at large, but only throughout the Invisible Church.

While the world will be left wondering about the absence of millions of people at one time, they are apparently not too shaken up by it to offer explanations that satisfy the average earth dweller, as is evidenced in other passages. However, when the Lord returns as shown in the Matthew passage, it *will be seen by everyone.*

As if seeing the eternal, all-powerful Son of the Living God appearing in the sky is not enough, the heavens will declare His presence with shaking, darkness, and a loud trumpet call. He will have everyone's attention! How anyone can think these two events are one in the same is beyond me, yet it is done by people who prefer to allegorize the text when there is nothing in the text that warrants allegorizing.

The reality of course is that in the I Thessalonians 4 passage, Paul speaks of no signs that are to occur prior to the Rapture. It is described as being imminent in that it could happen at any time. Nothing needs to take place prior to the Rapture in order for it to occur. This is not so when the Second Coming is described, either by Paul, or by Christ. There are signs prior to this event and the signs will be noted by the entire world. If one stops to think about, how could it be otherwise? The Creator is arriving back to His Creation to set up His rule and it is going to be an event which no one notices? They may not have noticed His arrival in His First Coming, but they will for the Second Coming.

Since the Rapture involves only the Invisible Church (those who are truly saved), there is no point in announcing it to the world. Except for the absence of millions of people, nothing else is seen by the world or presented to them by way of explanation.

For those who are left behind, but have heard the teaching of the Rapture and have heard the gospel of Jesus Christ, but never received Christ as Savior, it is very likely that they will understand in an instant what occurred.

The Gospel of John

John 14 is another passage that references the Rapture, in which Christ tells His disciples, *"In my Father's house are many rooms. If it were not so, would I have told you that I go to prepare a place for you? And if I go and prepare a place for you, I will come again and will take you to myself, that where I am you may be also."* Here we can see that Christ is obviously not referring to His Second Coming, which as we have seen in Paul's epistle to the Thessalonians, is a spectacle that the entire world will behold...and mourn.

In this particular passage of the gospel of John, Jesus is enlightening His disciples about the Rapture; how He will come to get His Bride and return to heaven (Father's House) with them. (This cannot be the Second Coming, since in that event Jesus comes all the way to the earth to set up His Kingdom as Ruler and Judge of all the earth.) It is to this event that Paul refers in the Thessalonians passages, and it is of this event that he wants the believers in Thessalonica to be fully aware.

Gathered Together

There are a number of other insightful passages in Thessalonians, but one more should suffice. From Paul's second letter to this church, II Thessalonians 2:1, he states, *"Now concerning the coming of our Lord Jesus Christ and our being gathered together to him."* The use of the phrase "our being gathered together to him" harkens back to Paul's first letter to this same church, when he first described the Rapture to them.

Apparently since then though, others have come in and attempted to sow doubts, even pretending that what they were saying was from Paul himself (cf. II Thessalonians 2:2)! It is very interesting how in many cases, the "ink" had not even dried on Paul's letters and Satan was busy trying to negate it by using false prophets and other imposters. Paul was well aware of the tactics of the enemy and did his level best to instruct the recipients of his letters to be aware of those same tactics as well. In this passage, Paul is again stating the fact that Christians will be gathered together to Christ. This obviously then refers to our meeting Him in the clouds, as Paul previously mentioned to them. He is not describing or discussing the time when Christ returns to this earth in judgment. He is talking about Christ taking His Body (or Bride; Church) off the earth and away from the *coming wrath*.

The difference is easy to spot when we look at another passage in II Thessalonians in which Paul declares, "*since indeed God considers it just to repay with affliction those who afflict you, and to grant relief to you who are afflicted as well as to us, when the Lord Jesus is revealed from heaven with his mighty angels in flaming fire, inflicting vengeance on those who do not know God and on those who do not obey the gospel of our Lord Jesus. They will suffer the punishment of eternal destruction, away from the presence of the Lord and from the glory of his might, when he comes on that day to be glorified in his saints, and to be marveled at among all who have believed, because our testimony to you was believed.*" (II Thessalonians 2:1-12)

It is evident (or should be) from this text that Paul is talking about the time when Jesus *comes to earth in judgment*, not to call His Bride out of the earth to meet in the air. Verse ten specifically states that His saints are already with Him when He returns to the earth in judgment. We are already glorified, and therefore will have already stood before Him in the judgment of our works, to determine which of our works will survive the fire and which crowns we may receive because of it.

Pre, Mid, Post or What?
John Walvoord elucidates further on the subject by stating, "*The exegesis of 2 Thessalonians 2:1-12 is a crucial aspect of the debate between posttribulationists and pretribulationists as both claim that this chapter makes a major contribution to their point of view. The matter is complicated because the interpretation and exegesis of this passage*

depend considerably on the interpreter's comprehension of the detailed prophetic program involved in the end-time events, climaxing in the second coming of Christ."[69] Walvoord then goes on to discuss the various interpretations of this chapter and concludes by stating, *"At the outset, posttribulationists have a real problem here. If the Thessalonians had been taught post-tribulationism, the beginning of the day of the Lord would have been to them evidence that the Rapture was drawing near and should have caused rejoicing. Instead of this, the beginning of the day of the Lord apparently created a panic in their midst, with the implication that before the false teachers had come they had understood that they would not enter this period."*[70]

Paul comments that the Thessalonian believers were wrong in the way they were thinking. The Day of the Lord had not already occurred. There had been absolutely no evidence that it had. As mentioned at the beginning of this chapter, it is important to understand the *language*, *history*, and especially the *culture* of the times when the Bible was written.

Gentile Christians do themselves and the Bible a huge disservice by not understanding the Jewish culture during the time of Christ (or during the Old Testament), as it plays a remarkably important part in providing a more complete picture of the actual meaning of the biblical text.

Marriage of the Lamb

By the same token, Jewish-Christian commentators like Dr. Arnold Fruchtenbaum provide a tremendous service to Gentile Christians with many of the works they have published. These detail the many ways that Judaism and Jewish culture play such a prominent role in the Bible. Gentile Christians too often forget this, to our own detri-

---

[69] John F. Walvoord, The Rapture Question, (Grand Rapids: Academic Books, 1979)
[70] Ibid

ment. A case in point involves the marriage process for the orthodox Jew, which includes four parts:

1. the arrangement of the marriage by the father;
2. the groom fetches the bride;
3. the wedding ceremony;
4. the marriage feast.

When all is said and done, and the Bible is studied in such a way that takes into consideration the language, history, and culture, and then it is allowed to interpret itself by comparing the whole of Scripture to itself, it is difficult if not impossible to come away with a confusion regarding the Rapture and the Second Coming. These each have their own place in the program of God.

The Rapture is clearly seen as a distinct event, separate from the Second Coming, which occurs at the end of the Great Tribulation period. Of this there can be no doubt.

Chapter 14

SLAVES IN EGYPT

Higher critics of the Bible tend to specialize in casting doubt regarding the veracity of Scripture. Their claimed success is dubious at best (depending upon how their information is interpreted), yet they persist in spite of the many, many times they have shown to be in error. Like the atheist and evolutionist, they keep plugging along.

There have been many cases too numerous to mention here that repel the false accusations of the critics. Unfortunately, in spite of any and all overwhelming evidence to the contrary, these enemies of God and those who follow and accept their rhetoric as gospel, persist in their attempts to demean, castigate, and otherwise downplay the believability of Scripture.

Of late, one of the more interesting assertions put forth by the critics is that the ancient Israelites were never in Ancient Egypt, especially as slaves. In other words, though the Bible provides a short overview of the 400 years they spent in Egypt, the critics contend that there is absolutely no proof that these historical events took place and consequently the biblical narrative is nothing more than myth, simply intended to teach moral truths.

There are a number of things that work against the claims of the higher critics, and the one thing that tends to work in favor of those who understand the Bible in literal terms is a little science referred to as archaeology. Archaeology unearths what has often been hidden for years, decades, and even centuries.

It is always fascinating when theories espoused by those who are purported to be scholars are upended by the recent discovery of a previously unknown document, statue, civilization, temple, or some other archaeological find, which sheds new light on a subject previously thought to be myth.

Such is the case with the Israelites' sojourn in Ancient Egypt. Is the information we have now enough to change the opinion of the critics? Of course not, but if we can legitimately silence them, then the new information is certainly worth it.

While there are some who state without hesitation that no proof exists of thousands of Hebrews leaving Egypt en masse, there is nothing that proves that it did *not* occur as well. In other words, we cannot use "silence" in the historical, extra-biblical record as proof that the events prior to and including the Exodus did not occur. It can be argued for instance that - *if the biblical account is correct* - the Egyptians would not be so quick to note such a major defeat (of Pharaoh and his army drowning in the Red Sea), in their own records that would become part of history. After all, each Pharaoh is equivalent to a god in Egyptian culture. It would not look good to include the fact that the God of the Hebrews called Pharaoh out and ultimately destroyed him. It would simply not look good at all, and given the fact that many kings of old, including Pharaohs tended to brag about their own exploits (often to the exclusion of *facts*), it would not be unheard of for this chapter in Egypt's history to be ignored altogether. The reasons for ignoring these events, or even whitewashing them would be to the Egyptians' best interest. What king or Pharaoh in his right mind would leave a record of history in which he looked bad? This was certainly not an uncommon practice and it is even done in modern times, with people rewriting history in order to make it more appealing to the masses.

In light of all this though, what if anything do we have that may support the biblical history of the Hebrews? Did they live in Egypt? Did they originally thrive there under Joseph, only to fall prey to a Pharaoh who knew nothing of Joseph? Was this new pharaoh threatened by the Hebrews' large numbers, forcing them into slavery because of it, until such a time as God brought a deliverer to them?

While there is a large area that could be covered, space here will not permit it. However, it is hoped that for the individual who seriously wonders about the plausibility of the biblical account, such a person would view this chapter as merely a starting point. There are many references - both on the Internet and in printed format - which address the time the Hebrews spent in bondage to Egyptian rulers and many of them are quite in depth.

There is a great deal in the Exodus account (as in much of the Bible) that bears consideration. In Exodus 1:11, we are told specifically that the rulers of Egypt ""*put slave masters over (the Hebrews) to oppress them with forced labor, and they built Pithom and Rameses as store cities for Pharaoh.*"[71] The first question then is did the cities of Pithom and Rameses actually exist? If they did, do we have record of it? Moreover, would we be able to place a date on when these cities existed? These are extremely important questions for obvious reasons and because the existence of these cities is embroiled in debate, some scholars have gone so far as to say that these cities never existed. However, let us turn to archaeology to see what, if anything, it can tell us...

According to the Archaeological Study Bible (Zondervan; 2005), archaeologists have located a number of sites which may well be the sites of the cities of Pithom and Rameses. The Pithom sites include three potential candidates.

1) Tell er-Retaba: The modern city of Tell er-Retaba is considered to be the most likely location for the city of Pithom. This is due to its proximity to the Nile Delta (just to the eastern edge) and roughly 60 miles east-northeast of Cairo. This is the only major fortified city in that entire area. This particular city is known to have been occupied during the Egyptian New Kingdom period of their history and this is generally believed to be the time of Israel's oppression and eventual exodus from Egypt.

2) Tell el-Maskhuta: If we travel just a few miles east, this modern day city is considered by some to be the ancient city of Pithom. However, this is ruled out by most scholars due to the fact that this particular city was "occupied only later, during the eighteenth to six-

---

[71] Exodus 1:11 (New International Version of the Holy Bible; Zondervan Publishing)

teenth centuries B.C., during the latter part of the Egyptian Middle Kingdom and the early Second Intermediate periods."[72] While it can be shown that Semitic people did live in this city because of shards of pottery unearthed as well as other artifacts, it is more consistent with the fact that these people were likely related to the Hyksos and not of Hebrew origin.

Though Tell el-Maskhuta is by some considered a candidate for the city of Pithom, scholars and archaeologists essentially believe that this city was abandoned from the 16th century to around 610 B.C. At that point, it was rebuilt under the direction of Pharaoh Neco II.

3) Hierapolis: This modern day city is also a candidate for Pithom; however Hierapolis is generally thought to be the city of On in the Old Testament (Genesis 41:50; Ezekiel 30:17).

Of the possible choices for the city of ancient Rameses, many scholars believe Qantir is likely the best choice, according to the Archaeological Study Bible. This is due to the ancient Egyptian records which refer to the city as having been on the waters of the Ra, which was on the easternmost area of the Nile Delta.

Archaeology has discovered that many Semitic peoples lived in this area and were generally referred to as "Asiatics by the Egyptians."[73] Tanis, the other consideration, is probably *not* the city of Rameses because of the dates associated with that city, which would place it well past the accepted date for the Exodus.

Another piece of potential evidence favoring the biblical text is the Soleb Hieroglyph. Amenhotep III of the 18th Dynasty built a temple

---

[72] Archaeological Study Bible, (Grand Rapids: Zondervan Publishing, 2005), 86
[73] Ibid, 86

in which archaeologists have found what they believe to be the first reference to YAHWEH outside of the Bible itself.

The hieroglyphics found at the temple *"memorialize Amenhotep III's domination of foreign peoples; subjugated peoples are depicted with their arms bound behind their backs."*[74] Whether or not it is true that he subjugated many foreign people is certainly open to debate, however what is *undeniably true* is the fact that one inscription in particular refers to *"the land of the Shasu, (those of) Yhw."*[75] Scholars are almost in universal agreement that the letters *Yhw* refer to Yahweh, Israel's God. If this inscription does indeed reference the Israelites, we can infer from this that the exodus from Egypt to Palestine took place prior to the time of Amenhotep III. Most biblical scholars believe the exodus occurred right around 1445 BC, which would have been approximately 50 years before Amenhotep III became Pharaoh.

Certainly nothing that has been mentioned thus far provides proof without equivocation, but the evidence does provide us with pieces of a puzzle that could well point to the full picture, once all the pieces are discovered.

The one piece of evidence that has been discovered and cannot be ignored is the inscription bearing the reference to Yhw. This no doubt refers to the God of Israel - Yahweh and because we know when Amenhotep reigned, we know that this name was used by a people who existed during that era.

Of three known Pharaohs of Egypt - Rameses II, Thutmose III and Amenhotep II - only the latter two are serious contenders for the Pharaoh who ruled during the Exodus, and this is based again on the archaeological evidence uncovered. Thutmose III is believed to have

---

[74] Archaeological Study Bible, (Grand Rapids: Zondervan Publishing, 2005), 86
[75] Ibid, 86

been the Pharaoh who built a store city on what later became known as Rameses. It is then possible that either Thutmose III or his son, Amenhotep II could have been the Pharaoh ruling during the Exodus, due to the time frames.

One other note of interest that points to a possible proof of the biblical exodus has to do with what has been found in June of 2003. It is very possible that at least one chariot wheel has been discovered at the bottom of the Red Sea. Of course there is controversy because only pictures of the wheel have been seen and unfortunately, the Egyptian government has now prohibited researchers from going down to actually obtain and remove any artifacts that might be there. How would it look if it could be proven with modern discoveries that Egypt's leader and army from a bygone era were literally overthrown by the God of Israel, especially considering the tension that exists in the Middle East today?

So in the end (which is really *not* the end, but merely the end of this chapter and book), what do we have? We have possibilities that could eventually lead to a final verdict. Should we jump on the bandwagon and say with all certainty that the proof is out there, so to speak? No, and for those who need the proof, it is likely that nothing will serve as final proof. At the same time, it is impossible to say with certainty that there is no proof of Israelite/Hebrew bondage in Ancient Egypt. While evidence suggests that the biblical account is true, the jury is still out.

For the Christian, a jury is not needed to determine that God's Word is just that - *His Word*. Because it is His Word, it is authentic, accurate and authoritative. It does not need to be defended against the attacks of so-called higher critics and certainly no amount of proof will convince anyone who does not really want to be convinced that the Bible is in fact, accurate. It serves to support the idea that God is in control and whether or not humanity believes in Him, or the history that is written in His Word makes no difference.

People routinely deny God's existence, His creative acts and His sovereignty. None of these denials however changes the fact that He *does* exist, He *has* created and He *is* sovereign.

While You Live and Breathe
As long as you are living, as long as you are breathing, as long as you are aware of your surroundings and can reason, you have time to receive the only salvation available to you.

If Jesus as God, did in fact take on the form of a Man, lived a sinless life, and died a sinner's death, the reality is that *you* do not have to do so.

Jesus spent more time talking about hell than anything else. It is a real place. All sin and evil will be thrown there. Anything and everything that is offensive to God will be removed from His presence for all eternity. Those who exchange their unrighteousness for Christ's righteousness will be saved. It is that simple and it does not get any more simple.

If I saw your house burning and you were trying to get back into it to save a photo album or some other inanimate object, I would do everything within my power to keep you from getting back into that house. If I did not, how could I call myself a caring human being?

I am asking you to consider the validity of Christ's invitation. God says all who die without Christ *choose* hell. The atheist says *"Don't worry about it. It won't happen."* The trouble is that they have not gotten past this life yet, so who are you going to believe? Please respond to His invitation by gladly receiving the salvation that He has made possible; that He has provided...for *you*. Please.

NOTES

RESOURCES

Christian Apologetics:

- *All the Messianic Prophecies of the Bible*
    - Herbert Lockyer (ISBN 0-310-28091-5)0
- *Answering the Objections of Atheists, Agnostics and Skeptics*
    - by Ron Rhodes (ISBN 0-7369-1288-6)
- *Commonly Misunderstood Bible Verses*
    - by Ron Rhodes (ISBN 0-7369-2175-3)
- *Coming to Grips with Genesis*
    - Mortenson & Ury (ISBN 978-0-89051-548-8)
- *Creation and Blessing*
    - Allen P. Ross (ISBN 0-8010-2107-3)
- *Every Prophecy of the Bible*
    - John Walvoord (ISBN1-5647-6758-2)
- *Faith Has Its Reasons*
    - K. Boa & R. Bowman, Jr. (ISBN 1-932805-34-6)
- *Gospel According to Jesus, The*
    - John MacArthur (ISBN 0-310-39491-0)
- *Hell Under Fire*
    - Morgan & Peterson, Editors (ISBN 978-0-3124041-9)
- *Jesus in Context*
    - Bock & Herrick, Editors (ISBN 0-8010-2719-5)
- *Reasons We Believe (50 Lines of Evidence...)*
    - Nathan Busenitz (ISBN 1-4335-0146-5)
- *Six Days of Genesis*
    - Paul F. Taylor (ISBN 978-0-89051-499-3)
- *Stones Cry Out, The*
    - Randall Price (ISBN 978-1-56507-640-2)
- *Temple and Bible Prophecy*
    - Randall Price (ISBN 978-0-73691-387-4)

- *You Can Lead an Atheist to Evidence...*
  - Ray Comfort (ISBN 978-1-935071-06-8
- *What Does the Bible Say About...?*
  - by Ron Rhodes (ISBN0-7369-1903-1)

Made in the USA
Charleston, SC
19 January 2010